# FLORIDA'S
# FAMOUS**ANIMALS**

# FLORIDA'S
# FAMOUS**ANIMALS**

True Stories of Sunset Sam the Dolphin, Snooty the Manatee,
Big Guy the Panther, and Others

## J G Annino

**g**pp

Guilford, Connecticut

Photo credits: p. 3 © by Dean K. Jue, 2006. All rights reserved.; pp 11, 18 Mike Ewen/*Tallahassee Democrat;* p. 28 Photo courtesy © Homosassa Springs Wildlife State Park/Bill Garvin; p. 37 p. 28 Photo courtesy © Homosassa Springs Wildlife State Park; p. 47 Clearwater Marine Acquarium; p. 55 Tampa's Lowry Park Zoo; p. 59 Sarah Eichler; p. 65, 70 Courtesy Halifax Historical Museum, Daytona Beach, Florida; p. 74 USGS, Sirenia Project, J.P. Reid; p. 87 South Florida Museum/Parker Manatee Aquarium; p. 95 Photo courtesy of Lee County POA Authority; p. 103, 106, 125 State Archives of Florida; p. 112 Photo by Larry O. Lansford; p. 199 Courtesy of the author.

Illustrations: pp. viii, ix, xi © Anna Annino; pp. 8, 68, 99 © Nova Development Corporation; all others © Dover Publications, Inc.

Text design by Deborah Nicolais

Library of Congress Cataloging-in-Publication Data is available on file.

ISBN 978-0-7627-4136-6

Printed in the United States of America

10 9 8 7 6 5 4 3 2 1

# CONTENTS

# TAKE A BOW (WOW!)

First an easel for Anna Annino, lifelong Floridian; chef to Ginger, the ladder-loving cat; high school student; and a community volunteer, for her spur-of-the-moment amazing animal line drawings on the dedication and introduction pages.

Florida is a land of many animals that help humans. It's also filled with folks who like to help. For assistance in locating animals and their stories, finding snapshots, for providing chow or companionship, and for insisting that Sunset Sam be included in these stories, I send a purr and a splash to Anna; to others in my family, especially Paolo, Joanna, Evelyn, and many cousins; also, to: Jody Taylor and Lichgate House volunteers who keep alive the story of Laura Jepsen and the Lichgate pooch, Kip (officially, Champion Fearnaught's Ace); Regina Lewis; Ann Morrow, Debra Katz, and M. R. Street; editor Megan Hiller, with whom I share affection for wild rabbits at Hollins University; Gia Manalio, Deborah Nicolais, and Diana Nuhn; all the generous animal owners, caretakers, and researchers interviewed; and also Sarah Carey, Larry Lansford, and Beth Powers; Stephanie Rutan; Florida Room, State Archives of Florida; Florida Photographic Collection/Florida Memory Project; Joan Morris; Adam Watson; The Florida Historical Society; Debra Galloway and Mike Ewen, *Tallahassee Democrat;* Manly Fuller and Preston Robertson, Florida Wildlife Federation; Henry Cabbage; Betsy Knight and the

Big Bend Wildlife Sanctuary; Janie and Ron Nelson; Holli, who keeps good stories about sweet dogs Sasha and Tasha; Dean Jue; Sandy Beck and the St. Francis Wildlife Association; Monica Ross; Nancy Kost; Chifuyu H. Beckett; Iske L. Vandevelde; Judith Delaney; Carolyn Self-Sullivan; Susan Strawbridge; Sarah Eichler's 2005–2006 second-grade class at Frontier Elementary School; Rachel Nelson; Holly Hall; Kelly Foster; Mike Weinberg; Rebecca Stansifer-Haggie; Laska Ryan, Barbara-Anne S. Urrutia, and Susan Saunders; Liliam Hatfield, who shares Miami Beach images with the world; Mitchell Green, who shares Florida books; Susan Stratton; Allen Thompson and Downtown Marketplace, Tallahassee, which offers animal education and stories through the St. Francis Wildlife Association every Saturday in season; Jan Collier; Leon County Animal Service Center/Pet Partners, which also shares true heartfelt animal tales every Saturday in season at Downtown Marketplace; Leon County Humane Society; the Tallahassee Spay & Neuter Clinic; Brooke, a future vet-in-training who is an inspiration to much older animal advocates; Georgia and Gracie, who love Maggie, the dog who wanted to go to school; and Joy, a teen who translated her love of animal stories into action. Big barks, perfect purrs, sunrise squawks, cool clicks, good growls, to animal advocates everywhere.

Finally, I especially want to remember in Sarasota, Riverview High School marine biology master teacher Ed Taylor. With passion and creativity he invited his students to consider the wide world pulsing in our fragile waters.

# DEDICATION

*These true stories are dedicated to Betty Mae Tiger Jumper, who as a girl in Florida refused to skin rabbits for the campfire stew, raised a crane from an egg snuck under a broody hen, and taught her pets to be part of a peaceable kingdom.*

# INTRODUCTION:
# MANATEES, PANTHERS, AND BEARS, OH MY!

In Oz Dorothy and her pals chanted, "Lions and tigers and bears, oh my!" In Florida we whisper, "Manatees and panthers and bears, oh my."

It's just a whisper because our manatees, panthers, and bears find their habitat crowded by people in Florida's race to become the third most populous state. Fortunately, some animal advocates also lend a hand to our threatened and endangered creatures. This book offers ample ways for students and families to connect with education programs and become involved in wild-species survival and domestic-animal rescue.

You'll meet some true celebrities here, twenty-three real, named animals that made history in Florida. Some still make news. Most chapters give you tips on where to visit a public site associated with the historic critter, or how to see that animal today.

Florida boasts a menagerie of famous animals in the wild, at zoos, or at home with people. How did I pick and choose which ones to include?

# Introduction

I've felt the moment was enchanted when a small herd of manatees, including mama and calf, slipped underneath me as we glided in a canoe on the Wakulla River. So I wanted to honor wild manatees. And I knew Snooty would join wild manatees in this book, because Snooty swam over to me when I was a teen. Chessie is a manatee for the record books. Just as with us uprights (what my cat Ginger calls us humans), some critters that made national headlines and the record books were naturals for *Florida's Famous Animals.*

In the Gulf of Mexico at Fort Myers Beach, I've floated stock-still while a dolphin fished directly toward me in table-flat clear water. And since I moved to the state in 1966, I've witnessed the leaps of uncountable numbers of wild dolphins in coastal waters. I couldn't forget Flipper, the movie and television name of at least five dolphins of my childhood. And my daughter lobbied for Sunset the dolphin, fondly remembering her visit to Clearwater Marine Aquarium years back.

A drama in Florida animal history took place in a small park between the two state agencies most responsible for the safety of Florida's wild black bears, when a yearling bear that was chased by people through Tallahassee took his last climb before capture, up a large oak tree in that downtown park.

Rosie is an animal I cried about when researching this book. What, oh, what became of Rosie? Let me know if you hear something solid about Carl Fisher's sweet and steady

Miami Beach worker, who apparently spent her last days in a traveling circus, after some time in Atlanta.

Jet is the pet I smiled about most. Left by owners in an animal shelter more than once, Jet dodged a death sentence to become one class act. He was so dedicated in clearing flight zones at Southwest International Airport in Fort Myers of big birds, which can take flight at the same time as jets, he even wanted to herd alligators when the birds weren't around. You'll have to read his story to see what happened with that.

So here are the animal tales. Entertainment, tears, laughter—the stuff upon which the best relationships, especially the human-animal kind, are made.

Let's go greet them.


P.S. If these stories inspire a student poem, artwork, or report in any format, please give us a bark at:

The Globe Pequot Press
Reader Response/Editorial Department
P.O. Box 480
Guilford, CT 06437.

editorial@GlobePequot.com

# MAYA: MYSTERY OWL

On March 12, 2004, a beach tourist on the sugar sand resort island of Perdido Key tucked away in Florida's far north Panhandle found an unlikely souvenir. A brown bird flapping in the roadway of Gulf Beach Highway close to Gulf Shores, Alabama, caught the attention of a driver. The unknown tourist stopped to observe a beautifully marked tiny owl struggling in the street. The bird couldn't fly. It was clearly hurt. The kind-natured visitor scooped up the bird, about the size of a fluffy kitten, and brought it back to the rental condo. As news of the injured owl spread, it was carefully passed along to someone who knew what to do.

The wild owl that had been flying to who knows where from who knows where, became a resident of the non-profit Wildlife Sanctuary of Northwest Florida at Pensacola. Its volunteers care for more than a hundred animals that can't return to where they came from in the wild, after they are discovered very sick or seriously injured. Beaver, deer, fox, golden eagles, bald eagles, hawks and, in this case, an owl, are on the list of formerly self-sufficient dinner guests who became permanently dependent on humans for their daily feed.

The wildlife care community is a tightly knit world of net-working professionals and volunteers. Soon, news of the owl reached Sandy Beck, an award-winning public school teacher of gifted children in North Florida at Tallahassee and a licensed wildlife educator.

Ms. Beck was interested in obtaining a new owl for The Wild Classroom, a popular outreach program using perma-nently disabled native animals in North Florida, of the St. Francis Wildlife Asso-ciation, which, like Wildlife Sanctuary of Northwest Florida, cares for a variety of injured or sick creatures.

*Audubon of Florida Center for Birds of Prey, Adopt-A Bird, including owls: www.audubonof florida.org/who_centers_ CBOP.html.*

So after the owl's treatment for a head and wing injury in Pensacola, the bird rescued from the road became Ms. Beck's ward, in exchange for another raptor, a Mississippi kite that could not be released to the wild.

Up until this time, the owl was considered to be one of Florida's little eastern screech owls, the smallest Florida owl, about as tall as a ketchup bottle. But, an owl with a big voice.

"However, when we removed her from her travel cage and I looked into her dark brown eyes for the first time, my mouth dropped," Ms. Beck remembered. She nearly screeched: "This is a flammulated owl!"

Flammulated owls are usually only about half the weight of tiny screech owls. They also have totally dark brown eyes, unlike the eastern screech owls' lighter eyes, and shorter

ear tufts. Because of reddish feathers, this species of owl is named for flames—*flammulated.*

Flammulated owls live west of the Rocky Mountains, far off from flat Florida. They aren't native to Florida or neighboring states.

Education volunteer Barbara Sullivan named the new mystery owl Maya. Maya weighed 130 grams, about the weight of a kitten.

Maya began adjusting to her new world. She met two eastern screech owls already in residence at The Wild Classroom. More differences became apparent.

As Maya met with visitors late one afternoon, she swiveled her head and curiously looked around from her perch on Ms. Sullivan's gloved hand. "Look at her. She's inquisitive," said Ms. Sullivan.

Ms. Beck agreed. "That's right. Screech owls just want to blend in. Screech owls are the proverbial wallflower. They want to sit and look like a branch. They want to hide. Maya won't do that," said Ms. Beck, who was also thinking ahead to doling out that night's thawed white rat to each one of her several raptor residents.

It wasn't long after Maya's transition to Tallahassee, when news of the new bird that was possibly a screech owl but possibly not, flapped its way around the binoculars crowd. Dean and Sally Jue, a well-known Florida birding couple representing the Florida Ornithological Society, flew across town to see the odd avian. Maya, seeming to bask in the attention, patiently posed for enough photos to complete a portfolio that would be shared with the birding world.

In Dean Jue's photograph of Maya on page three, you can see Maya's big dark brown eyes that clearly differentiate her from those of screech owls. A little harder to detect but still apparent, are the differences in ear tuft size. Maya's ear tufts are smaller than a screech owl's. Although

# Owl Oddities

- The burrowing owl is the helicopter of Florida birds; it can hover in mid-air. This species likes to be out and about in the daylight, compared with usually night-hunting owls.

- The flammulated owl species that mysterious Maya *may* be related to, often likes a dinner of rats, squirrels, moles, snakes or bats. In the world, there are 150 owl species; in North America, 19.

- Who put the screech in screech owl? Not everyone hears a screech when a screech owl speaks. Listen to three sample calls at www.owlpages.com/sounds.php. Scroll down to Eastern Screech Owl. And best of all, hear Maya the mystery owl sing digitally at www.wildclassroom.net/photos/raptors.html.

captivated by the curiosity of this owl, the Jues reserved judgment on Maya's species.

Gary Graves, research scientist and curator, department of vertebrate zoology at the Smithsonian's National Museum of Natural History in Washington, D.C., was keen to look at Maya's photos and listen to Maya talk on a digital recording. "This is definitely a strange bird," said Graves. "Based on the photographs you sent," he wrote Ms. Beck in an e-mail, "if it weren't for the unusually large body mass, I would have no problem considering it to be a flammulated owl."

Graves said solutions to the mystery of Maya could be that she is an unusually fat flammulated owl, or an exotic species of Scops owl that normally doesn't occur at all in North America, or a screech owl with brown eyes, which would be bizarre because there has never been such a brown-eyed screech owl on record, or, a hybrid between the western screech owl living west of the Rocky Mountains and the flammulated owl.

"I have studied these sorts of phenomena for thirty years. This is indeed an interesting case!" the Smithsonian curator wrote Ms. Beck.

The interest did not stop there. Photographer Lincoln Karim, from New York City, known for photographing that city's celebrity red-tailed hawk, Pale Male (the subject of a popular documentary movie *Pale Male),* learned about Maya while on assignment in Florida. He photographed her gorgeous big dark eyes, adding Maya to wildlife photographs at the Pale Male Web site: www.palemale.com.

*Like Harry Potter? Well then how about Hedwig, Pigwidgeon, and even the owl dastardly Draco has? Find out more about the Owls of Harry Potter at The Nature Conservatory's site: www.nature.org/initiatives/programs/birds/features.*

Maya's fame was growing. Then added interest blew in across the oceans from Australia, where the operators of The Owl Pages, (www.owlpages.com) posted a photograph and information about Maya's mystery on the site's Unusual Gallery page.

In other ways Maya is quite normal for an owl. As a primarily nocturnal creature, she perks up at night. "She just sings all night long," said Ms. Sullivan, "although I'd really call it more of a gargle."

On many Saturdays Maya met with fans at the St. Francis Wildlife Association's education booth in Tallahassee's seasonal Downtown Marketplace. Added flutters of attention came her way the summer of 2006 with the release of the movie version of Carl Hiaasen's Young Adult Fiction novel about burrowing owls in Florida, *Hoot.*

And for Ms. Beck, using the Maya puzzle is a great way to teach taxonomy. Taxonomy is the way science groups, or classifies, living things. Until a few years ago both screech and flammulated owls were listed in the same genus, *Otus.* But the taxonomists decided to reclassify them, because of their difference in bird calls and their mitchrondrial DNA. Only animals that share the same genus can successfully interbreed, such as polar bears and grizzly bears were famously found to have done in the wild in 2006.

Since the attractive avian's arrival in The Wild Classroom, Maya's story has prompted other owl experts to give

# Owls that Naturally Prowl in Florida

| Common Name | Scientific Name |
| --- | --- |
| Barred | *Strix varia* |
| Barn | *Tyto alba* |
| Burrowing | *Athne cunicularia* |
| Eastern Screech | *Megascops asio* |
| Great Horned | *Bubo virginianus* |

If Florida weather is foul, look for these out-of-state owls:

Long-eared
Short-eared
Northern Saw-whet
Snowy

a hoot about her origins, with their comments, posted at the Owl Pages decidedly on the screech owl side of the nest.

What is Ms. Beck's best guess? She wonders if Maya is the result of a wild bird fling between a flammulated owl and a screech owl. She also thinks rough weather could have blown this unique offspring off course (Flammulated owls migrate to Central America and *The Field Guide to the Birds of North America* published by the National Geographic considers the flammulated to be an accidental Florida visitor). Only DNA from a molted feather will tell for sure.

*Real Florida burrowing get their chance to shine onscreen in the popular movie* Hoot, *adapted from Carl Hiaasen's Newbery Medal–winning novel (New York: Random House, 2002).*

Everyone who gives a hoot about the survival of birds, especially unique owls such as Maya, will always be grateful for an unknown tourist who slowed down while on vacation for a bird in distress.

# DAVE: PARADE CAT

Everyone loves a parade. But not every cat does. And then there's Dave.

The booms of band drums, the whinnies of horses in mounted posse, and the clatter of motorcycle units can give a cat the creeps. It's no wonder cats hide out from parades.

But not Dave the Cat. He never let a bit of parade noise or bustle deter him from having a quiet, good time. In fact, Dave the Cat led parades, much to the delight of North Florida children and visitors.

His trick to enjoying a parade? He rode snuggled on top of the shoulders of his human, who became known as the Catman.

Dave the Cat developed such a fan base in twelve years of public appearances, the local newspaper published comments of praise from fans as far away as California who watched Dave the Cat glide by in a parade when visiting the state: "A parade does not seem complete without you. . . . The Catman is back, which thrilled my daughter. The sight of a man riding a bicycle with a cat was both amazing and unique."

Like many cat tales, Dave's story begins with a scratchy start. In fact, it begins with a near-death sentence. As a kitten he was brought to a public animal shelter in Atlanta. Fate intervened in the form of Peter Holtmann, who adopted the tabby, a gray and white fluff ball.

In the meantime, about 230 miles south in Tallahassee, Florida, a computer expert named Mitch Gans, a college student who loved to ride his bicycle, wanted a new cat pal to love after the passing of his beloved cat, Elliot.

Holtmann heard of his friend's request and decided to give Gans the cute kitten he had recently adopted. It was love at first meow, shortly after New Year's Day of 1988.

*Known as the nation's largest animal sanctuary, the Colorado-based Best Friends Animal Society (www.bestfriends.org and publisher of Best Friends Magazine) rescued at least 6,000 pets, including many cats, after Hurricane Katrina hit states along the Gulf of Mexico in August 2005.*

Within days when Dave the Cat saw Gans come home from classes at Lively Technical Center, the kitten scampered up the student's side or back to lie across his shoulders. It was as if Gans was a fine tree and Dave had found the perfect branch for a cozy stretch.

But this tree moved. It didn't bother Dave. As Gans did chores around the apartment, Dave stayed happily on his shoulders, purring contentedly.

Soon Dave the Cat ventured outdoors on Gans's shoulders. Then when Gans rode his bicycle on Tallahassee's tree-lined back streets, Dave the Cat rode, too.

"He would just see me coming down the hall and he would jump up my back to get to my shoulders. He was ready to go," Gans explained of the immediate alliance the two formed.

Just three weeks after arriving at his new home with Gans, Dave the Cat entertained thousands at his first parade, just by lying draped across Gans's shoulders.

# Here, Kitty, Kitty

- An estimated thirty million pets are house cats, *Felis catus*.

- To handle a flying fur ball of millions and millions and millions of cats, an image made famous by the artist Wanda Gag in her beloved children's tale, *Millions of Cats,* it's best to make sure your kitty is unable to reproduce. For information on free and low-cost spay and neuter sources, contact your vet or local humane society and animal shelters. As Abraham Lincoln said: "No matter how much the cats fight, there always seem to be plenty of kittens."

- According to the respected 4 Paws cat rescue group of Merrifield, Virginia, one—just one—unspayed female cat and her first offspring, left unspayed, can reproduce nearly 400,000 cats in seven years.

People peered at Gans as he moved along the route and would wonder: *What does that guy have on his shoulder?* When Gans drew closer and they saw the cute little cat, people cheered. Few folks had seen a house cat in a parade before.

As a supine feline, Dave the Cat charmed Florida's Senator Bob Graham, a former Florida governor and the parade marshal at Dave the Cat's first parade. This was the Springtime Tallahassee Parade of March 26, 1988.

After that Dave the Cat became a fixture at many events, from Veterans Day affairs, where Gans somberly wore all black and attached a flag to his bicycle, to jubilant college parades in Tallahassee, home to Tallahassee Community College, Florida Agricultural & Mechanical University, and Florida State University. Dave the Cat also appeared at winter carnivals, Dr. Martin Luther King Jr. Day parades, inaugurations of governors, a library dedication, and a watermelon festival, and he traveled to Birmingham, Alabama, for a pet festival.

*Fun feline facts: www.fourpaws.org, www.hsus.org.*

"He just seemed to love the crowds. And they loved him," said Gans, who would some- times dress as Tweety Bird and Dave would be—well, he would be Dave the Cat.

Dave never jumped off Gans's shoulders into the crowd, nor by his behavior did he ever ask to leave. He didn't act intimidated by attention from well-wishers who would walk over to meet him during a pause in the parade.

Gans, who was also a popular local pizza chef and amateur mime, became known as the Catman. People who saw Gans and Dave together said they both had a sparkle in their eyes.

A newspaper pet columnist published a piece about the duo. Local and state officials posed for photographs with Dave the Cat, including another Florida governor, Bob Martinez.

As you can guess, part of the success of this unique parade act lay in the human part of the team. Gans once had befriended a three-legged cat, Tigger, who of course required special care. Gans also organized his town's only mime troupe and developed a devoted following wherever he cooked in town. During a power outage after Hurricane Elena in 1985, Gans and waitress Claudia Belleware gamely showed up for work. In the dark they managed to crank out pizza with the gas ovens and serve the meal by candlelight. Another time Gans left his chef's duties at a small music hall to provide an hour-plus of impromptu entertainment when the power failed. Surely Dave the Cat sensed something special in Gans, the Catman.

Sadly, after nearly seventeen years of living with Gans, Dave stopped eating.

Then began a series of trips to the vet and treatments. Whatever was wrong with him took Dave the Cat's life on July 3, 2004. (Most cat-age conversion charts show that three cat years equal twenty-one human years, eight cat years are about forty human years, and fourteen cat years of life equal seventy human years, so Dave the Cat was truly old.)

Gans never renewed the parade-cat concept that had been the crowning glory of his friendship with Dave, though the rescued shelter cats who live with him and his wife — Clyde, Gourd, Gracie, Jasper, Jethro, and Squash—all seem to have a sparkle in their eyes, too.

# Cats, International

| | |
|---|---|
| Arabic | *kitte* |
| French | *chat* |
| German | *katze* |
| Italian | *gatto* |
| Japanese | *neko* |
| Spanish | *gato* |

# BOO BOO: CAPITAL BEAR

On a hot August night in 1996, a yearling black bear scurried down a tree in the backyard of a south-side Tallahassee neighborhood. Resident Suzanne Allen later told the newspaper that she watched from inside, amazed, as the wild bear padded from the oak tree toward her small house.

"He literally got up to the window and put his nose up to the window," a surprised Allen said in an interview.

In response to the bear's curiosity, Allen did something she never would have imagined. She walked to the window and put her fingers up to the glass, matching her hand to the bear's paw that rested on her windowpane.

The bear stayed put.

Then she leaned in to put her eyes close to the glass. She peered out at the bear; for a bit it stayed, looking in.

The bear watcher came away from the window feeling sorry for the bear. "He's tired and worn out," she told the newspaper.

Allen's unlikely face-off wasn't the town's first sighting of this bear. For days, neighbors of the Greenleaf area in south Tallahassee, a leafy community of mainly modest rental and

longer-term homes with some commercial sites along the Woodville Highway, reported to wildlife officials visits of a small, wandering black bear. It didn't turn over trash cans or seem to be interested in human food.

Florida bears are considered unaggressive, normally shy. "They keep to themselves. They don't look for interactions," said the state's bear program coordinator, Stephanie Simek.

Wildlife experts who arrived on the scene to glimpse the bear said it appeared healthy and weighed about 150 pounds. They said it was lost from the nearby Apalachicola National Forest, a bear territory that begins just 10 miles from Florida's busy Capitol Center Complex. They guessed the yearling recently had been pushed from the forest home of his youth in a normal seasonal eviction, sent away by a combination of his mother and older, competitive males.

Because the bear had padded into town from the forest, located just two to three miles south and west of town, officials hoped it would find its own way back. The rural nature of the neighborhood, with clumps of tall, inviting pine trees, must have at first looked good to the bear in search of a new home, especially if it arrived during the quiet, inactive night.

But dogs barked and chased. By day, understandably curious neighbors inched closer for best views. This attention made it a bear on the run, seeking the next tree, where it climbed and again clung on, waiting for the commotion to subside.

Each time the bear was discovered, the ruckus began anew as word spread among neighbors about the cute young bear in their midst. Happy neighborhood children soon gave it a name—Boo Boo Bear.

After a couple days of successive tree climbs that never brought it to the right new territory, followed by dashes into nearby undeveloped and wooded lots, the bear changed tactics.

And that's how Suzanne Allen came to match hand to paw, face to face, with a wild bear. Boo Boo poked around Allen's house long enough for wildlife officials to arrive.

Hoping to send the furry guest back toward the forest, they shooed it away from the house. But Boo Boo climbed the nearest tree, which turned out to be a utility pole.

*Central Florida Zoological Park, near Sanford, offers an animal outreach program. The presentation features animals that share Florida black bear habitat: http://centralfloridazoo.org.*

"We thought we were going to have fried bear," neighbor Rita Jenkins told the newspaper.

Something about the pole must have seemed less than treelike. Boo Boo suddenly stopped climbing. He jumped down, ran through the yard and down the street, and disappeared into a thick patch of darkening woods at the end of the street. It seemed that he had skedaddled.

Instead, Boo Boo apparently had headed north into a hilly part of Tallahassee, capital city of the fourth most populous state, rather than southwest into the forest plain and flatwoods.

The next day Boo Boo nosed into the Myers Park neighborhood, a leafy and hilly historic neighborhood. This area is just a stroll from downtown and the state Capitol Center Complex, which has no statues of Florida bears but does boast a silvery sculpture of leaping Florida dolphins.

From the Myers Park neighborhood Boo Boo made his

way to a historic downtown green space called Cascades, considered to have once been the site of flat Florida's genuine town waterfall, which exists no more.

By now, after days of publicity and with on-the-scene reports spreading fast, Boo Boo Bear's moves kept a parade of the curious, police patrol cars, and wildlife officials moving, too. This was a bear on the run—with a crowd following.

# Gentle Ben

In 1967–1969 a trained actor bear from California, Bruno, lived in South Florida to become the animal star of a popular television series filmed in the state. *Gentle Ben* (Bruno's television name) told the exploits of an Everglades-dwelling bear. Guest stars on the show included Florida native son Burt Reynolds. Dennis Weaver played Bruno, Ben's owner, an Everglades National Park ranger. Clint Howard, brother of director/actor Ron Howard, played the bear's child friend, and Clint and Ron's real-life dad, Rance Howard, played the part of a backwoodsman. In one celebrated episode, Bruno-Ben performs in the water with a Florida dolphin, known as Flipper, from the popular television show of the same name. (See Flipper at the end of the "Sunset Sam" chapter.)

The annual Florida Black Bear Festival is in Umatilla, Florida: www.floridablackbearfest.org.

As he monitored the situation from his office downtown, state wildlife official Tim Breault heard a surprising comment on his telephone, from a wildlife biologist who was following the bear on foot: "He's going to the Capitol!"

At the same time, Breault heard sirens near his downtown office building. "I looked outside my window and my jaw just about dropped. Right from my window I saw the bear run right into the park across the street," Breault remembered.

The park Boo Boo ran into is a grassy and wooded green space that connects the downtown wildlife building

# Ol' Slewfoot/Tim

Another Florida bear-actor lived at the Piper Everglades Wonder Gardens in Bonita Springs in southwest Florida. Tim the bear was filmed as Ol' Slewfoot, a bear in the movie version of the coming-of-age tale *The Yearling,* by one of Florida's celebrated writers, Marjorie Kinnan Rawlings. The Yearling won the Pulitzer Prize in 1939. Her Cross Creek farmyard and home south of Gainesville are a National Historic Site.

parking lot and the parking lot for the nearby road building agency. Each of these agencies has the important work of helping protect Florida's bears.

Breault saw a patrol car screech to a stop. He watched the officer jump out, take his bicycle from the rack, and ride into the park after Boo Boo.

Police, the curious, and wildlife officials found Boo Boo perched quietly up in a tree, seeking safety.

"It was a great big live oak tree," recalled wildlife biologist David Johnson, who with wildlife biologist Richard Crossett had the task of ending Boo Boo's visit to town.

A crowd of about 150 onlookers stood below Boo Boo, including office workers of the state wildlife agency, some of whom had never seen a wild bear before.

*Big Bend Wildlife Sanctuary has rehabilitated at least seventy-two bears back into the wild. The folks at the sanctuary make educational visits, too. Contact them at (850) 762-8685, bbwsi@digital exp.com, or RRI, Box 255K, Altha, FL 32421-9784.*

As six to eight people held a Tallahassee Fire Department tarpaulin beneath the live oak tree, Boo Boo received a dart of muscle relaxant.

He fell directly into the outstretched tarp. Next he was bundled into a waiting pickup truck.

By 1:00 p.m. that day, his chauffeurs reported that Boo Boo was back in the 750,000-acre Apalachicola National Forest, an Eden of springs, sinkholes, and trails in sandy pine woods, naturally filled with nuts, berries, and other bear chow.

After years of allowing Florida's dwindling bear population to be hunted, Florida halted bear hunting in 1994. Because of that, as far as anyone knows, Boo Boo—the bear who visited a state capital city—lives in the forest today. He will always be remembered as a quiet, wild bear who spent several days in town wandering among humans and lived to learn from his experience.

# Bear Bits

The Latin or binomid, name of the Florida black bear is *Ursus americanus floridanus.*

Young Florida black bear cubs are eaten by bobcats, coyotes (in North Florida), or adult male bears.

Bears are threatened by traffic and by development of bear territory. In 2003 111 bears were killed on roads; in 2004 the bear deaths climbed to 127.

The colorful "Conserve Wildlife" Florida vehicle license tag features the Florida black bear.

# **B**ears on the Beach?

Your chances of seeing a wild black bear in Florida increase when you visit these bear habitats:

- Collier-Seminole State Park: www.floridastateparks.org/collier seminole/default.ctm
- Everglades National Park: www.nps.gov/ever
- Big Cypress National Preserve: www.nps.gov/bicy
- Ocala National Forest/Wekiva River Basin: www.fs.fed.us/r9/florida
- Osceola National Forest: www.fs.fed.us/r8/florida
- Apalachicola National Forest: www.fs.fed.us/r8/florida
- St. Marks National Wildlife Refuge: www.fws.gov/saintmarks

Outstanding sites with captive Florida bears provide public education in exchange for permission to keep bears. They include:

- Tallahassee Museum of History and Natural Science: www .tallahasseemuseum.org
- Jacksonville Zoo: www.jaxzoo.org
- Lowry Park Zoo, Tampa: www.lowryparkzoo.com
- Naples Zoo: www.napleszoo.com
- Brevard Zoo, Melbourne: www.brevardzoo.com
- Central Florida Zoological Park, Sanford: www.centralflorida zoo.org

# ELECTRA: MANATEE AIDED BY MANATEES

It was a spring Saturday like many others at the Fish Bowl. The natural pool is a lively part of an Eden of clear springs that sparkle in Florida's central west coast, north of Tampa. They create a celebrated state marine conservation region, with the historic Homosassa Springs Wildlife State Park sparkling as the star of the area.

Late afternoon at the state park is the time for the last talk of the day about manatees that live there. Manatees are the gigantic but gentle, slow marine mammals, 1,200 pounds or more, that need warm water because of their sensitivity to cold temperatures.

*Electra is not the only manatee SeaWorld–Orlando nursed back to health: www.seaworld.org/animal-info/info-books/manatee/index.htm.*

Manatees can't rotate their heads and must turn their entire bodies around to look behind them. In busy Florida they can't seem to get out of the way of boat traffic. The Florida manatee, a subspecies of the West Indian Manatee, is federally listed as being endangered, with a federal study suggesting in 2007 that the status could be downgraded.

*The best up-to-date reference on all things manatee,* The Florida Manatee: Biology and Conservation, *by manatee experts Roger Reep and Robert Bonde, was published in 2006 by the University of Florida Press: www.upf.com.*

Visitors who had met the park's twin Florida black bears, Brutus and Biddie, rescued years back from Ocala National Forest, and had visited with other critters now climbed up into metal bleacher seats. They looked down upon the spring waters and hoped a swimming manatee, one of the park's resident herd of six females, would meander over in the water.

A wildlife ranger, Matt Robinson, stood in the water up to his hips, wearing leg waders. As he spoke to the visitors, Robinson shared the good, the bad, and the ugly involving Florida's manatees.

When these herbivores, or plant-munchers, graze on bottom seagrass beds, they leave a tell-tale "swirly footprint" on the surface as they glide through water. You can look for these footprints on the water surface to spot manatees below.

For their super size, manatees are fragile, with lungs that are susceptible to pneumonia, like human lungs. Only their paddle tail propels them, not the flippers. So they can't speed out of the way of boat hulls and propellers. They are snagged by other human-created hazards, such as discarded fishing line, which is illegal to toss, but few people

are prosecuted for the violation. So as long as they share the same waters as humans and their hazards, manatees can be torn into, rammed, snagged, and then wait for infection to set in, or they can be mortally wounded on impact.

Habitat loss, water pollution, and a natural event of harmful algal bloom, or HAB (previously called Red Tide), also hurt the population. For example, in 1996 one HAB in the Gulf of Mexico caused manatees' lungs to bleed and sent toxins into their brains, killing 415 manatees.

As Robinson spoke, a manatee at first out of sight of the crowd, named Electra, undulated her large tail paddle ever so slowly to swim over to see if the two legs under the water were connected to a bucket with a treat for her. They were. Electra slowly turned over underwater, showing her belly to visitors who snapped photographs.

In December 1998, on the opposite coast of Florida in the Indian River lagoon, this very same manatee had been badly injured in a boating accident. After the smash-up, wounded and disoriented, she eventually had become entangled underwater in fishing lines that had wrapped around her right flipper. This manatee had open wounds to her lungs and diaphragm, making every breath a challenge. It seemed as if she would suffer a slow death alone.

But over the years Florida's children have made the manatee the official state marine mammal. They have joined with popular education programs, such as the Save the Manatee Club, to educate the public about the help manatees need. Back in December 1998, someone reported this manatee's trouble. Florida's dedicated

*A longtime nonprofit group, Save the Manatee, champions protection efforts and offers manatee adoption kits: www.savethemanatee.com.*

marine mammal rescue system is coordinated among state and federal officials, volunteer vets, nonprofit marine science centers, and commercial marine parks, such as the popular SeaWorld in Orlando.

Soon the severely wounded manatee won a free ticket to stay at SeaWorld.

# Sewer Sam

In 1969 a soon-to-be famous Florida manatee got stuck in a sewage pipe in Miami. Contractors were shocked to find a 1,200-pound, 9-foot manatee wedged entirely inside a storm-sewer pipe that ran under West Dixie Highway at Northeast 163rd Street in a construction project.

With difficulty and amid much publicity, the manatee was tugged out of the culvert. In the process it was nicknamed Sewer Sam, a silly name inappropriate for the situation. The mammal was near death, lacerated, badly bruised, and malnourished.

Fortunately the Miami Seaquarium's veterinarian, Jesse White, and crew were able to free him. Later ocean explorer Jacques-Yves Cousteau became intrigued by Sam's story. And so in 1971 this manatee was flown via C-46 cargo plane 260 miles north to Three Sisters Springs at Crystal River, near Homosassa Springs. For two weeks he acclimated to the natural environment and food sources. An underwater gate kept him in the spring. Once outfitted with a tracking device, Sam was set free from the spring. He lingered near the spring but later was seen swimming with several other manatees. He may still be out there swimming, although his signals stopped transmitting. He became famous when Cousteau released "The Forgotten Mermaids" segment of his popular television series, *The Underwater World of Jacques Cousteau,* which featured Sam's amazing story and release.

# Electra: Manatee Aided by Manatees

It still wasn't certain she would live. SeaWorld staffers cared for her. They cleansed her wounds, stitched her up, gave her medicine and nutrients with tube-feeding and watched her carefully for signs of infection.

Electra survived the accident, transfer, and aftercare. She went from a low of 765 pounds to 900. But it became clear that the diaphragm and lung muscle injuries had hurt her ability to be buoyant, to rise to the surface to breathe. Every manatee must do this to live.

Electra developed a unique technique of positioning her body as vertically as possible underwater, tail down, supporting her full weight on that tail paddle. This allowed her whiskered snout to break the surface for life-giving breaths.

Electra's inability to swim to the surface made her an ideal candidate for Homosassa Springs. It has both deep water and shallow areas. The 45-foot-deep first-magnitude spring, headwaters of the Homosassa River, flows to the Gulf of Mexico. But the deep areas are bordered by small, shallow spring-fed lagoons. In May of 2000 Electra got a free ticket to the state park. She joined the park's captive manatee herd, as a manatee unable to survive in the wild.

*Follow manatees with the U.S. Geological Survey Sirenia Project. See wildtracks.org, http://soundwaves.usgs.gov and sirenian.org.*

Soon the staff observed something curious. The female manatees would nuzzle up against her, pushing her toward the surface. And that helped her to breathe.

# Manatee Moments

- Florida's manatee is *Trichechus manatus latirostris.*

- The order that includes manatees is *Sirenia,* meaning "sea cow."

- The Florida manatee can live in both fresh and salt water.

- Important manatee tools are their bristly body hairs, called vibrissae, which send them messages about what's in their watery world.

- Manatees' tiny eyes are contained in dimple folds of skin. New research is showing that manatees probably can distinguish color and that their brains are more complex than people originally realized.

If Electra drifted into deep waters, the herd matriarch, named Rosie, would gently position herself under Electra. That lifted her to the surface, or brought her drifting back to shallow water.

"Rosie's behavior was very maternal. She would go upside down and lift Electra up with her flippers to breathe," said Robinson. Rosie continued helping Electra in this fashion until Electra healed, regaining her ability to swim to the surface.

"They have a strong will to survive," Robinson said of Electra's journey back to unassisted breathing. "Her confidence level is going up more and more."

That day at the end of Electra's visit and Robinson's presentation, a student in the Q&A session said she thought boat propellers should be covered, like electric fans. But that's no longer a solution. Monica Ross, senior researcher in St. Petersburg with the Wildlife Trust and Manatee Rehabilitation Partnership, said propeller guards, which at first were thought helpful, actually can produce a greater impact, even breaking manatee ribs.

Afterward, as visitors walked along the park's waterside subtropical paths to watch other manatees that hadn't joined the program, two visitors stopped to look out over the natural clear-water pool and ponder what they had just seen.

"It's just amazing," said Marianne Hughes, of Peterborough in central England. "We don't ever get the chance to have manatees in England. The people here are so lucky, so lucky, to have this on their doorstep. I'm not sure they appreciate it."

*The agency responsible for protecting manatees is the Florida Fish and Wildlife Conservation Commission: http://myfwc .com/manatees.*

"I think it's magical," her husband, Neil, said about Electra's boat hit, entanglement, near-death rescue, and fine healing with a little help from human and manatee friends.

"I think," said Marianne Hughes, "that manatees are more sensitive than some humans are."

## You Can Visit Electra!

Electra, Rosie, and their herd of manatee pals live at the lush Homosassa Springs Wildlife State Park in Citrus County, north of Tampa (www.homosassasprings.org, www.hswsp.com, and www.floridastateparks.org/homosassasprings).

# LU: TOWN HIPPO

Far out west in California, a pair of African hippos, Rube, the dad, and Lotus, the mom, became parents with the birth of their baby boy. The hippo born to them in 1960, at the San Diego Zoo, weighed 90 pounds, a mere river rat in size compared to grown ups, because male hippos can bulk up to 7,000 pounds.

This baby arrived safely during an underwater birth, the way all baby hippos enter this world. Very quickly Lotus pushed her boy up to the surface to take his first breath.

This little hippo was not destined to remain on display with his parents. You can imagine how cute he was, with chubby cheeks, big round black eyes, and tiny round ears. He was so cute he became a young movie star. He went to work for Ivan Tors, a famous animal trainer who created movie and television shows that featured animal actors along with the human stars.

Tors worked in California but he also set up shop in Florida, making movies and television shows such as *Flipper*, about a dolphin, and *Gentle Ben,* about a Florida bear in the Everglades. And that's how the young hippo became a resident of Florida. According to records of the

San Diego Zoo, he arrived at Homosassa Springs Wildlife Park, then a private zoo, when he was six years old in 1966. Today in Florida, where he is a famous citizen, he is affectionately known as Lu. (For something on other Tors animal actors, see the end of the "Boo Boo" bear chapter to read about Gentle Ben, and the end of the "Sunset Sam" chapter for information on the dolphin called Flipper.)

The whiskered water-lover Lu spent winter in west Florida with the animal actors group at the private animal park, near the town of Crystal River. Lu was the group's only hippo actor. But his kind are social animals. And Lu was without a hippo to bond with. So he became fast friends with an actor donkey named Susie. Lu followed Susie the donkey everywhere. In fact it was known that if an animal handler wanted to have Lu do some work, or simply move to another area, Susie had to go first, and Lu would follow. This was a fast friendship much like the famous bond that developed between a one-year-old hippo in Kenya known as Owen and a 130-year-old giant tortoise known as Mzee, after a tsunami made Owen an orphan in December 2004.

Lu the hippo had lots of work as an actor. Once he was seen in living rooms all across the country as the star of a Union Carbide television commercial, where he tossed around a tire with his jaws. On camera the tire didn't rip, despite the pounding Lu gave it. Today one of Lu's favorite toys still is a tire, which he likes to rest his head upon underwater or push around his brown pond in the lush gardens at Homosassa Springs Wildlife State Park at Crystal

■ Visit hippo Owen and giant tortoise Mzee online at www.lafargeecosystems.com, the Web site for Haller Park, Mombasa, Kenya. Meet Owen's new hippo pal, Cleo.

■ For information about the Owen and Mzee movie, released in coordination with Scholastic in 2007, visit www.owenand mzee.com.

■ At least two picture books also document the famous friend-ship. They are *Owen & Mzee: The True Story of a Remarkable Friendship* and *Owen & Mzee: The Language of Friendship,* both by Isabella Hatkoff, Craig Hatkoff, and Dr. Paula Kahumbu, with photographs by Peter Greste. New York: Scholastic/Turtle Pond Publications, 2005, 2007.

River on Florida's central west coast. Lu's newest tractor tire was a birthday gift from his fans at Homosassa Tire.

Lu also appeared on several television variety shows. But his big work came in the late 1960s when he had recur-ring roles in episodes of the Tors television show *Daktari.* The show was an evening drama about the fictional Wameru Study Center for Animal Behavior in East Africa, where large hippos like Lu live. (Smaller, solitary, pygmy hippos are found in west Africa.) Many *Daktari* episodes centered on dangers to Africa's amazing animals, such as illegal hunt-ing, called poaching.

So forty years ago Lu was part of early attention drawn to the plight of the exotic wild species of Africa. Today Lu still is an ambassador for hippos.

Lu turned forty-seven years old in 2007. Every year Homosassa Elementary School students, town residents, and Florida tourists celebrate Lu's birthday with a big party at the park.

Nancy Kost lives in the area. She loves how much the community adores their town hippo, Lu. "He's not supposed to be there, because he's not native, but everybody thinks he's so cute," she said.

For every birthday, which park officials celebrate in January, Lu can expect a big cake and a new toy. The cake is actually bread baked up to look like a cake. Once it was baked in the shape of an actor's star. The frosting is real. Lu usually eats all of his cake. The human visitors receive treats too, such as hippo-decorated cupcakes. People sing "Happy Birthday" to Lu and learn a lot about hippos.

Although baby hippos can swim, adult hippos like Lu are too dense to truly swim. So Lu pushes off from the bottom

## You Can Visit Lu!

Before you visit Lu, who is featured daily in a 12:30 p.m. education presentation, be sure to visit him online at Homosassa Springs Wildlife State Park Web sites: www.homosassasprings.org and www.floridastateparks.org/homosassasprings

of his pond with webbed feet and then lands, to push off again in a sort of water dance as he maneuvers around his small pond. At other times you can see him lumber up on a solid landing, to hold still for a welcome mouthwash from a water hose. But even with his mouth closed, it's hard to miss his curved tusk. Another bit of inside information: Avoid being close to Lu's enclosure fence when he is out of the pond and about to fling his poop, called dung. His warning signal is his backing up to his wall and quick tail spinning. The park even sells T-shirts that brag, "I survived the Splatter Zone at Homosassa Springs."

Though Lu is the park animal with the longest confirmed residency, it wasn't always certain that he could live there to the end of his days. Hippos can live to be about fifty in the wild. A hippo named Donna in Indiana was at least fifty-five. Lu's mother, Lotus, died when she was forty-five and his father, Rube, died at age fifty-two.

Non-native Lu and other exotic critters had faced a big trip years ago. In 1989 the park went from private ownership to inclusion in the State of Florida's network of award-winning natural parks. The network emphasizes Florida's natural heritage, so new homes had to be found for the exotic animals.

People in Lu's town were bothered about the challenge Lu might have in moving, and about the idea of having to travel to some unknown place, possibly far away, to visit Lu. So they wrote many letters to convince officials to keep Lu, who, after all, had moved in as a six-year-old.

The many requests finally reached all the way to the office of Florida Governor Lawton Chiles. In 1992 he said he wished that Lu would "live peacefully at home in Homosassa Springs." And Lu has stayed put ever since.

Through the years Lu the actor has mugged a bit, to become perhaps the park's most-photographed resident. "Almost 300,000 guests come to visit the hippo every year, making him an important part of the Florida Park Service and local community," said park manager Art Yerian.

One of Lu's newest fans is Miles Gray Clarke, who lives near Niagara Falls, New York, and made his first visit to Lu as a two-year-old in 2006, with his grandmother, retired

# **H**ip Hippo Sites

- Looking for ways to save the hippo? Visit www.savethehippo.com.

- Looking to listen to what a hippo sounds like? Visit www.awf.org.

- Or maybe you are looking to keep up with the members of the international hippo club, Hippolofus, and check in on Lu himself? Visit www.hippos.com.

- You can see Kito, a baby hippo, and mom Moxie at Busch Gardens. www.buschgardens.com.

Dunkirk, New York, schoolteacher Lynn Clarke. She is a devoted Lu fan.

Lynn Clarke, also known as "CJ," is so fond of Lu, she and her family included visits to Lu on their Florida vacations from New York State. In retirement she and her husband, Michael, moved just an hour away from Lu, in Leesburg. Lu was the first live hippo CJ had ever seen up close. Watching him eat during a Florida vacation with her husband and two youngest sons, Aaron and Benjamin, more than fifteen years ago, she said she experienced hippo love that has lasted ever since.

"He flipped his ears around, and he usually just did that when he was coming out of the water," she said. "But he didn't have water in his ears, just peanuts in his mouth! When he chewed and chewed and chewed, his eyes would close in pleasure. When he opened them again, we could marvel at his big brown eyes and his long curved lashes."

Lu's huge appetite has pushed his estimated weight up to an impressive 6,000 pounds. Every day he chows down on fourteen pounds of alfalfa hay, in special blocks, special scoops of vitamins and nutrients for herbivores—plant-eaters like Lu—and he empties a five-gallon bucket of its yummy vegetables.

In 2005 for Lu's forty-fifth birthday party, CJ and her family bought cantaloupes for Lu, which his keepers saved for welcome treats later. CJ has also visited Lu as part of an international club of hippo-lovers. In October 2005 during

# **M**ore Highlights for
## *Hippopotamus Amphibious*

- Called *kiboko* in Swahili, this animal gets its name from the Greek words for *hippo*, meaning horse, and potamos, referring to river. So the ancient Greeks, who could look at hippos on the island of Cyprus, thought of them as a river horse (although we know today they aren't horses). New research shows that their closest relatives are actually cetaceans, or whales, and not pigs, as once also believed.

- Hippos are the second or third largest land mammals, after elephants. Specialists have a friendly disagreement about whether hippos or white rhinos are the second largest.

- Hippos are poor swimmers! But they can walk submerged on river bottoms for up to six minutes before pushing off from the bottom for a gulp of fresh air.

- In modern times hippos have become locally extinct in Egypt.

their annual meeting in Florida, called a Hippopalooza, eighteen club members learned about hippo behavior from park wildlife care specialist Susan Lowe and park vet Dr. Kenneth Lowe, her husband.

"Lu has fans all over the world," said park spokeswoman Susan Strawbridge. This big guy is so popular, reports about him are posted on the hippo club Web site, where handsome Lu mugs for the camera.

# SUNSET SAM:
# DOLPHIN DEEDS

One day in May 1984, a reporter called the Clearwater Marine Aquarium, a responder to marine animal emer-
gencies. Did the staff know there was a dead dolphin in
nearby Tampa Bay, within a hop, skip, and a jump of the
nonprofit waterfront center? No one knew.

The aquarium's skiff soon skimmed across the water
with staff on the lookout for the body. Near sunset, they
saw it, stuck on a mud flat. But when they approached, the
body moved. Despite being very weak, the animal tried to
swim. The dolphin was lifted onto a stretcher and rushed
first by boat and then by vehicle to a veterinarian for emergency care. It was badly dehydrated, scraped, sunburned,
and malnourished. Tests revealed that it was suffering from
pneumonia and parasites. Later it became clear the dolphin
was also visually limited in its right eye. Surely it would
have died during the night, if it hadn't been for the
reporter's call and the aquarium's rescue.

For the next year and a half, the aquarium staff and volunteer vet nursed the sick Atlantic bottlenose dolphin. It

Protect Dolphins Campaign, NOAA Fisheries Office of Protected Resources: *www.nmfs.noaa.gov/pr/education/ protectdolphins.htm.*

gradually improved, gained weight, even became very active, although it was nagged with a liver disorder that lingered. The veterinarian and staff knew that this dolphin would never be able to live safely back out in the wild. But how the creature ever got so close to death was still a mystery.

The mammal, one of Florida's most popular, perky symbols, became a permanent resident of the small aquarium's saltwater pools. In nearby tanks were sea turtles, small stingrays, and schools of mullet, among other species. The new resident acquired a name, Sunset Sam. The staff worked with Sunset Sam in a program of stimulation to try to keep him from being bored in the confines of the 17-foot-deep tanks of seawater. He became the small aquarium's first rehabilitated dolphin. Aquarium staff also discovered that he was considered the first beached, or stranded, dolphin in Florida known to survive such a harsh stranding.

Because the activities were set up as voluntary, he didn't always participate when aquarium visitors stopped by his pool for a look. But when he did, Sunset, as he came to be called, made a guest feel special. He was never taught to jump or dance or otherwise perform. If he wanted to, he would splash and jump. If he wanted to, he could play with favorite toys, such as a rope with a small buoy attached, which he liked to dive with. But he wasn't expected to perform.

One day former animal training director Melissa Koberna decided to offer Sunset the chance to do something he had never done in the wild—hold a paintbrush in his snout, dip it in paint, and make marks on a canvas. The result is that Sunset became a "painter," turning out abstract art that

SeaWorld—Orlando also offers Web pages of dolphin information, sourced by scientific studies: www.seaworld.org/info-books/Bottlenose/what-is-a-dolphin.htm.

was sold in the aquarium gift shop for $50 or was given away to nonprofit groups for fund-raisers. Once, Sunset's squiggles were featured in an online show of animal art. Another time one of his pieces was presented to former U.S. First Lady Barbara Bush. For Sunset, who took a rubber-tipped brush in his mouth about twice a week, it was a welcome variation in his activities, according to Koberna.

Dolphins haven't yet been documented to see color, but people saw shapes in the splashes Sunset painted on things. One of his pieces was entered anonymously in a local art show, and he won! But he was disqualified when the organizers learned the artist was an animal, according to senior trainer Abigale Stone.

Sunset also painted on T-shirts and hats. In a community campaign to place decorated sea turtle sculptures around town, he painted on a fiberglass turtle. If Sunset

The "Watch that Wildlife: Viewing Wildlife in the Florida Keys" brochure offers good tips on correctly observing wild Florida dolphins and other native species. See www.dolphinecology.org.

didn't want to paint when the brush and paint were brought out, he didn't.

While other sick, stranded, or injured dolphins came into the aquarium for care—such as residents known as Rudy; Autumn and her calf, Harvey; and CeSar—they were able to return to the wild. One of them was tracked swimming freely as far away as North Carolina.

Not Sunset. His permanent injuries kept him from going back to the wild.

The staff monitored his liver problem. He usually had a good appetite, eating about twenty pounds of food daily in the summer and about twenty-five pounds in the winter. Squid, herring, Atlantic sardines, and other saltwater delicacies were his favorites. He also took vitamins and calcium supplements.

Sunset was as long as a small, one-person rowboat— 9 feet, 2 inches long. When his health improved and he ate all that seafood, he eventually bulked up to about 500 pounds. He was gray and white and swam like a silver streak in the clear water. Some visitors would try to get a peek at him and Sunset would stay underwater the entire time. Others were delighted to arrive when he had decided to break the surface and jump in the three-hundred-and-fifty-thousand-gallon pool.

*Mote Marine Laboratory is an excellent scientific research center that participates in the world's longest ongoing dolphin study. The laboratory offers engaging student and public education programs and large aquariums on Florida's west coast at Sarasota. See www.mote.org.*

In 1992 Sunset began to help special children and teens who would benefit from private attention. He was part of the aquarium's animal-assisted therapy program, which included other marine residents such as Mo, a sea turtle with a shell birth defect who couldn't dive for food, and Splash, a stingray.

"He definitely responded differently to those children," said Stone. "With kids he just knew they needed extra help and he would give it. He would stay up out of the water longer to let them take rings off him. He was very attentive and interested in the kids."

Dolphins can be rough in the wild with each other—slamming into pod members and biting, for example. They can and do hurt humans who swim with them in the wild. No child was allowed to go in the pool. But Sunset could choose to come over to the side of the pool, where the child waited. A child who had difficulty with speech, for example, might be helped to learn words associated with Sunset and his activities. Because Sunset was permanently disabled with liver disease and nearly blind in his right eye, special-needs children could relate their own challenges to his when they helped care for the special-needs dolphin.

*Sarasota Dolphin Research Program—one of the world's longest-studied dolphin groups is in Florida: www.sarasota dolphin.org.*

The aquarium received national recognition from Mary Tyler Moore and the Delta Society in 1998 for this wide-ranging program of activities, called Full Circle. Soon news of Sunset and the other therapy marine animals at Clearwater Marine Aquarium put them in the spotlight, such as on Animal Planet, HBO, and with praise from animal celebrity Jack Hanna. More people wanted to see Sunset Sam at the aquarium than ever before.

# Flipper

The most famous dolphin name in Florida belonged to a movie and TV star—Flipper. At least five dolphins actually played the role of Flipper. The first one starred in the 1963 movie *Flipper*. Others shared the work in a second movie, *Flipper's New Adventure,* and they also swam and lept on a popular television show of the 1960s based on the movies. The idea of a helpful dolphin that rescued people and sometimes even helped their wayward pets appealed so widely, that for a time, the name Flipper became synonymous with "dolphin" or "porpoise" in children's minds.

The first Flipper was netted in the Gulf of Mexico near Marco Island in May 1961 by Milton Santini. His family called her Mitzi and taught her to carry people on her back. The four other dolphins who later shared the Flipper role were caught by the Miami Seaquarium. Mitzi, who may have been fifteen years old, died in June 1971 at Santini Porpoise School in the Florida Keys, reportedly of a heart attack. She will always be remembered as the first dolphin to bring international attention to the skills of this special species.

But in 2001 something was very wrong with the dolphin. He began losing weight. One day he scraped a gate in his tank. And sadly, by the next morning, December 4, 2001, he was dead. He had lived seventeen years past his stranding and he was thought to be twenty-two years old when he died. A memorial statement from the aquarium said, "Sunset Sam will be missed and we will grieve. His memory and the gifts he gave the world in general and each individual who ever saw him will outlive us all."

"He was just an amazing animal," said Stone, the senior trainer who worked with Sunset in the Full Circle program. "I still have visitors who arrive and say, 'What happened to Sunset?' He was so memorable. We all felt lucky to have him around for seventeen years."

## Nellie

The Marineland Dolphin Conservation Center on the coast south of St. Augustine is home to a dolphin named Nellie. As the state's very first marine attraction, Marine Studios opened in 1938 and introduced many people to their first captive dolphins.

The name changed to Marineland and became world-known. Today Nellie is the site's most famous dolphin. Marineland DCC celebrated Nellie's fifty-fourth birthday in 2007 with an ice-and-fish birthday "cake."

# Dolphin Discussion

- A dolphin is not a porpoise. Differences include the dolphin's longer snout and its spade-shaped teeth. Dolphins are in the family *Delphinidae,* while porpoise are classified in the family *Phocoenidae.*

- Surprisingly, dolphins probably hear most sounds primarily through their highly specialized lower jaw and secondarily through their ears, the subject of a lot of study.

- Sounds dolphins make underwater, including clicks, come back to them as sound waves, which help them navigate so expertly. This is called echolocation.

- Dolphins, which have two important kinds of eye cells, rods and cones, may be able to detect some color, although this hasn't yet been documented.

- Giant underwater fishing nets, called gill nets, are responsible for many dolphin deaths around the world. Dolphin-safe tuna signs on cans of store tuna represent some tuna fleet measures to limit dolphin killing.

- It is considered harassment to deliberately swim with or feed wild dolphins. They are protected by the Marine Mammal Protection Act of 1972.

# TAMANI: 205-POUND NEWBORN

At Tampa's Lowry Park Zoo, at the end of work on October 16, 2005, caregivers left the park with an animal nose count of about 1,700 creatures great and small.

Monday, October 17, 2005, the tally had inched up by one nose—a nose twenty-four inches long. This new nose at the end of a trunk belonged to an elephant that didn't exist on the planet the day before. Deep into that October night and most likely close to a rosy dawn, a mom-to-be elephant had given birth in the zoo. Tampa's newborn male elephant calf tipped the scales at 205 pounds at his first weigh-in. Next to his mom, a 7,250-pounder, the baby looked like a little elephant toy. His head wore matching floppy gray-brown ears—pink behind the ears—that he had no trouble beginning to flap. He looked out on the world with clear eyes, big and brown.

His mother, Ellie, a twenty-year-old first-time mother, and this unnamed baby were tended to during and immediately after birth by the zoo's female elephants. Elephants are highly intelligent creatures that collectively care for one another.

# Elements of Elephants

- In Latin *ele* means "arch" and *phant* represents "bigness."

- Tamani's nighttime birth is the custom of wild elephants. Such events remain among the least-documented aspects of their amazing lives.

- Elephants are undisputedly the largest land mammal on Earth.

- Tamani's kind, *Loxodonta africana,* once were in all of sub-Saharan Africa but now remain in only one-third of the continent.

- Most people think the illegal ivory tusk trade has ended. But in Chad, Africa, from May through October of 2006, conservationist J. Michael Fay, on assignment for *National Geographic* magazine, found that six park rangers were murdered while protecting elephants from ivory-takers. He also saw hundreds of bodies of dead elephants, tusks removed, outside Zakouma National Park. They had been shot by poachers for their tusks.

- In Asia people also are working hard to protect the smaller Asian elephant, *Elephas maximus,* which is native from India east through Vietnam.

"Though Ellie had no experience giving birth, she had other elephants close by who had experienced birth in Africa," said zoo veterinarian David Murphy after the baby's birth. "Having experienced caretakers is indispensable for a calf's growth and development." These female family members, acting as natural elephant allomothers, or aunts, are named Matjeka and Mbali. With Ellie they are raising him.

This newborn's arrival was unusual for several reasons. Because of elephants' size and wide migratory range, it is understood that these wild giants do best in vast protected territories where elephant families can work together. So fewer animals today are in captivity and even fewer give birth in zoos, leading to a lack of diversity in the captive elephant stock. In a zoo the birth of an elephant is an uncommon milestone.

A remarkable aspect of this baby's arrival involves exercises many human moms-to-be do. The baby's mom went through months of childbirth lessons given by the attentive zoo staff. Just as many human moms practice certain stretches and other exercises, mom-to-be Ellie had guidance in an elephant version of Lamaze training. Ellie was encouraged to stretch and squat so that when the baby arrived, she would want to squat, making the baby's natural fall from out of the womb to the ground shorter and less hard. Ellie also was encouraged to practice positioning her front legs so that it would be easier for the baby to reach up and find her mammary glands to nurse with his mouth.

And then to the great joy of schoolchildren, this baby quickly became the subject of a contest: What should he be named? Right away Florida children jumped into the name game. Many thought up perfect names. Hundreds of schools in the Tampa region turned in classroom suggestions after studying African elephants to learn how humans can help them. The students heard about the primary human language of the regions where the elephants live. They collected facts about what elephants eat in the wild and how they work together in elephant families.

The zoo staff thought about all the names submitted by schoolchildren and posted six schools' suggestions online for a public vote. Interest in naming Ellie's baby was so huge that eventually 10,607 individual votes were tallied, some from overseas. The name finalists included: Jabali, meaning "strong as a rock," suggested by Joanne DuPont's first-grade class at Maniscalco Elementary and by Vicki Womble's kindergarten class at Purcell Elementary; Moja, or "first one," from Katherine Frost and Tarrelle Brooks's fifth-grade classes at Muller Magnet Elementary; or Kidogo "something small," the idea of Joseph Piazza's seventh- through twelfth-grade classes at LaVoy Exceptional Center; Jasiri, or "fearless," from Sandra Hendrick's sixth-grade class at West Hernando Middle; and the winning name, "Tamani," for "hope," from first-year teacher Sarah Eichler's second-grade class at Frontier Elementary.

Although each of these beautiful names exactly fit this baby, who had turned out to have a very curious and frisky personality, Frontier's fine idea won.

Frontier second-grader Toby Amass was clear about the perfect match up of name with baby. "I like the name because it may help it live a long and healthy life. Tamani means a lot to me, because elephants are endangered," he wrote for a special class project. Classmate Alissa McCoy agreed. "We thought of the name," she explained in a special essay, "because we hoped elephants would not go extinct."

# You Can Visit Tamani!

- To visit Tamani first check the Lowry Park Zoo's Web site for updates on when Mom Ellie, aunts Matjeka and Mbali, and the young one most likely will be easiest to see: www.lowry parkzoo.com.

- You can see African elephants make a big splash in Florida at Jacksonville Zoo's Plains of East Africa elephant pavilion, with its peek at pachyderm doggie paddling, via the 275,000-gallon pool: www.jaxzoo.org.

- At Walt Disney World's Animal Kingdom, the Kilimanjaro Safari is the path to elephant sighting. The site's "Parks" button leads to Animal Kingdom information: http://disney world.disney.go.com.

- Asian elephants trumpet at Miami MetroZoo. For information visit www.miamimetrozoo.com.

Tamani officially received his name on Wednesday, December 21, 2005, with 550 school families and teachers attending the event at the baby's home.

In the weeks and months after birth, Tamani and his mom spent all their time in the very important work of bonding. As Tamani nursed, he doubled his size in just six months. He grew from a wrinkly newborn of 205 pounds in October 2005 to a wrinkly 500-pound toddler in April 2006.

In January 2007 he weighed nearly as much as a small car, 970 pounds.

Tamani is a mover and shaker. "Much like a toddler, he has a short attention span and he gets into everything," said zoo spokeswoman Rachel F. Nelson. One of Tamani's favorite things to do is to chase the free-range African guinea fowl that live in his home in the zoo. He also likes to climb over tree trunks on the ground and receive an adult-elephant push over a tree trunk when needed. He enjoys wallowing in mud, and he loves to eat.

For about three years Tamani nursed. He gradually began to nibble on grown-up chow that includes bananas, apples, and hay. He also tried oats, carrots, corn on the cob, and, a natural for an elephant in Florida, palm fronds.

Another achievement, other than adding solid food, was his mastery of the important skill of trunk tactics. His trunk has about forty thousand muscles in it, which should all be exercised. Watching his elders, Tamani learned how to inhale water up his trunk to spray it around and to release that water into his mouth for a drink. Although elephants pick up water with their trunks, they use their mouth directly to nurse. Tamani stood on a special seven-inch-tall platform so he could reach his long-legged mother to nurse.

Tamani has received top grades from zoo staff in all his baby elephant tasks, including from his primary human caregiver, Steve LeFave, assistant curator for African hoofs-tock. The caregiver became one of the most unusual campers in Florida when he slept in the elephant barn for

# Don't forget to check out these sites:

David Sheldrick Wildlife Trust:
www.sheldrickwildlifetrust.org

Elephant Care International: www.elephantcare.org

Elephant Trust: www.elephanttrust.org

World Wildlife Fund's pygmy elephant project:
www.worldwildlife.org

## Remember these sources too:

Helmuth, Laura. "Saving Mali's Migratory Elephants." *Smithsonian,* July 2005.

Kehret, Peg. *Saving Lilly*. New York: SimonSays/Simon & Schuster, 2000.

the first week of Tamani's life to help make sure things went well.

"He trumpets a little bit now," said LeFave. "He's started to do what's called a rumble, as a greeting, a happy greeting. Pretty much everything he does he learns from the grown-ups. They've taught him to dig holes. He can climb over trees lying on the ground."

What's ahead for Tamani is more big eating and playing. And for special birthdays such as his fifth in 2010, he can expect a giant cake made up of fresh veggies and fruit, hay, and bread during a big birthday party in Tampa for the elephant whose name represents hope.

# BROWNIE:
# DOG FOR ALL OF DAYTONA

mportant guests stood in a park with the mayor of Daytona Beach, looking grim that late October day in 1954. A Daytona Cab Company car drove up to the park. A door opened. With care, four men lifted a small hand-built coffin from the cab's backseat. In silence they carried the coffin to a beautiful site in Riverfront Park.

Mayor Jack Tamm presided over the funeral for a Daytona Beach resident: Brownie, the town dog.

"Daytona Beach has lost one of its finest citizens," said the mayor to the crowd of mourners, estimated at seventy-five people. Tamm said he hoped that "wherever it is that good dogs go, he [Brownie] has already arrived." The mayor called for a moment of silent prayer in honor of Brownie. And then the men lowered Brownie's coffin, which contained his embalmed body, into the newly dug ground.

The local newspaper, which devoted four photographs to the dog's funeral, summarized the event with this headline: MANY A DAMPENED EYE AS BROWNIE IS BURIED IN RIVERFRONT PARK.

Some dog! What was it about this dog that prompted

*Best Wishes for the coming year*

Brownie

humans to stage a send-off with a funeral and burial in a lovely public park?

Brownie's story begins in mystery. No one knows where Brownie was born or what his puppy days were like. It is generally agreed that "one day" in 1939 a new dog walked into town. This dog was large, quiet, and calm. He seemed willing to be petted by anyone who bent over to offer a scratch between his ears. The dog had none of the characteristics of a lost animal. He didn't act confused, scared, starved, or hurt. His hair was short and light brown. Some said he looked mainly like a Labrador retriever. Others said he must have had the heritage of the boxer, hound, or even Rhodesian ridgeback breeds. Whatever his parentage, this new dog in town wore no collar or ear tattoo. And 1939 was long before the invention of pet microchip IDs.

For a few days the dog wandered around the downtown Daytona Beach area on the mainland. He ambled along sidewalks and storefronts, collecting scraps of food from restaurants and new pals. He poked into back alleyways. He checked out the waterfront park, marina, and yacht club, which stretched invitingly along a tranquil lagoon of the Intracoastal Waterway, called the Halifax River. Just over the lagoon bridge and down a street lay Daytona's famous sandy beach and the beach drive, A1A, alongside the Atlantic Ocean, but the dog seemed to like the mainland.

Downtown locals commented about the dog. He didn't seem to belong to anyone. Several people now regularly fed him scraps, but the dog didn't stay with them. He liked everyone up and down the street and didn't seem to want to move on to anywhere else.

After a few days the dog clearly lingered longer on the sidewalk at a busy intersection. It was opposite the bridge that led from the mainland across the lagoon, to the beach side of the town and to the Atlantic Ocean. Most important for the dog, this was the corner where the awnings of the Daytona Cab Company taxicab stand provided a bit of shade. This intersection, where Orange Avenue and the mainland Beach Street crossed, became the dog's favorite place to doze when he wasn't walking around. And when it finally was time to sleep through the night, this was where the dog circled and settled down.

# See for Yourself!

Visit Brownie's bank, now home to the interesting Halifax Historical Society and Museum, 252 South Beach Street in Daytona Beach, also at www.halifaxhistorical.org. In Riverfront Park, see Brownie's grave and memorial topiary bush in an area of cafes, independent bookstores, and a magic shop, in addition to the museum in an old bank building (www.daytonabeach.com).

The downtown dog soon acquired a likely name—Brownie—a reflection of his light brown coat. Downtown regulars, especially Ed Budgen, one of the cab company's owners, cabdriver Gilbert Glessner, and business owner C. P. Miller, became involved in Brownie's regular care,

# Rescue a Dog

Florida is a state where dogs race around a track while people gamble on which dog will win, like in horse-racing. Some of these dogs later are put up for adoption, some at a very young age. The dogs have specific requirements which include an ideal family, with the time and money to see to their needs. But there are other ways to help in dog rescue. Information about these unusual adoptions is available:

Racing Dog Rescue Project: www.rdrp-greyhound.org.

Greyhound Adoptions of Florida: www.ahome4greys.org.

Greyhound Pets of America, Orlando: www.greyhound petsorlando.org.

making sure he ate and enjoyed a source of water, that he was issued an official dog license, and that he had shelter.

First his home was a big cardboard box under the cab company awning. Later on in the same spot he moved into a hand-built doghouse that had a sign, BROWNIE'S HOUSE. His new friends had him examined by a veterinarian, who estimated that the friendly fella was about a year old. But despite many people's care, Brownie wasn't their dog. "He was friends with everybody," historical columnist Robert Hunter wrote. Reporter Jack Troy wrote, "Never has a dog captured a town's heart as Brownie has in Daytona Beach." And Bourke Davidson told a reporter, "He was nobody's dog, but he was everybody's dog."

During the day Brownie walked up and down Orange Avenue and Beach Street by himself. After school, children sought out Brownie for a pat on the head or a hug around the neck. At night he followed a patrolman on his walking rounds of downtown.

If you have ever let a pet wander, you know that this sort of outdoor life is risky and unsafe. Brownie was hit by cars in the downtown neighborhood. One of those accidents gave him a broken hip, treated after he was rushed in a taxi cab to see the vet. Concerned visitors during his convalescence at the vet's brought Brownie steak. He eventually mended but kept a slight limp.

Brownie also was attacked by aggressive night-roaming dogs at least twice. After every incident, Brownie's vet bills

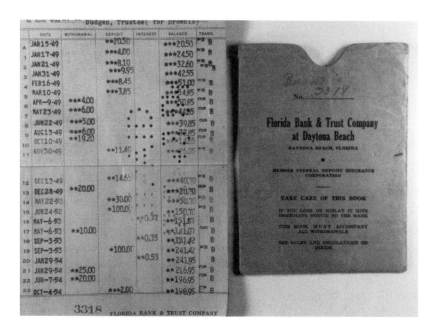

were taken care of by donations. By then a donation box for his needs was attached to his doghouse.

In winter glass went up in his doghouse door; in summer, like everyone else in the days before air conditioning, Brownie switched to using a screened door.

When Brownie's donation box filled, he took a walk a few doors down the sidewalk with a trusted human to the Florida Bank and Trust Company. Brownie likely was the only dog in Florida and one of the few, if any, in the entire country then to have his own bank account—No. 3318. Sometimes he needed spending money. One day in 1950 Brownie went to the bank. Then he continued down the sidewalk to a drugstore to buy a vanilla ice cream soda for himself and for Beauregard, a calf that was the son of a famous cow named Elsie. The bovine and the canine didn't become life-long pals, but each tolerated the publicity stunt.

That event was not Brownie's idea; it was staged to draw attention to the business Elsie and her calf, Beauregard, represented, the Borden Dairy Company. It also helped draw attention to Daytona Beach.

Even without visiting bovine celebrities, Brownie did a steady job of publicizing Daytona Beach. His human friends made up a photographic postcard of Brownie sitting next to his sidewalk house for tourists to mail back home. Brownie's humans also sent out greetings cards at Christmas for him. By then people from Maine to Texas sent Brownie money and mail. Feature stories about the sweet town dog of Daytona Beach had appeared far beyond Daytona Beach.

When visitors arrived in town, in addition to enjoying the famous beach and the promenade with a clock tower and band shell made of rare coquina rock, some also wanted to visit the mainland and meet Brownie.

Brownie remained Daytona's town dog from 1940 through 1954. It was then that a chronic bronchitis infection, along with recurring heartworms, took their toll. He was at least fifteen years old. He spent about twenty days under constant medical care in his vet's office hospital, with the newspaper providing updates on his condition. He died in his sleep at the vet's office.

Then cabdrivers Bob Robertson and Gilbert Glessner, two of his earliest friends, built a small coffin for the park funeral service.

Although the corner cab stand is long gone, you can still walk into Brownie's bank building, 252 South Beach Street. It is old and beautiful, dating to 1910, when it was built as the Merchant's Bank. Ask to look at Brownie's bankbook and to see photographs about the cuddly canine. The old bank today is the home of the Halifax Historical Society and Museum, which interprets the town's considerable history. Alone among Florida museums, it can boast about keeping the archives of Brownie, town dog. Then, staying alert for traffic, you can step across landscaped Beach Street for a stroll in Riverside Park. Enjoy the sight of a unique topiary sculpture, probably the only dog-shaped bush planted in honor of a real dog in Florida. Look for Brownie's shiny granite grave marker that says: THE TOWN DOG, 1939–1954, A GOOD DOG.

# CHESSIE:
# COLD-WATER VISITOR

In the summer of 1995 all along the coast of New England, little children raced into the water and splashed back out, yelling that it was just too cold. Then they plunged in again because it was summer.

A native Florida swimmer the size of a small rowboat also tested these same shoreline waters that August. This amazing warm-water mammal, looking like a giant swimming potato, was a Florida manatee. Normally it lived in Florida, but this manatee seemed to want to travel as far from home as it could. It had swum steadily north all the way about 1,500 miles, from Florida to Rhode Island.

Something in the rippling Rhode Island waters must have finally given this manatee a shiver. At a coastal region called Point Judith, known for its lighthouse beacon, the manatee turned around.

Some time between September 23, when it swam near Virginia, and November 16, when it was reliably spotted near Jacksonville, it had arrived back in Florida. And so this manatee, known as Chessie, officially entered the history

books in 1995 as the longest-traveled manatee in the world—some 3,000 miles up and back.

Even before he set a record for many leagues swimming the sea, Chessie was a famous face. The summer before, in 1994, this manatee was also seen far north of Florida in Maryland waters. That's when it was affectionately named Chessie, for a legendary Chesapeake Bay "sea monster" talked about at least a hundred years before.

# Chessie: Cold-water Visitor

In 1994 people worried about this new Chessie, resident of subtropical Florida, and a subspecies of the West Indian Manatee. Manatees live in warmer, shallow water, eat marine plants, and are among the most passive herbivores on Earth. They are famous for not being able to even turn their heads around to look at a boat bearing down on them. They have to turn their entire bodies. How would Chessie thrive in the autumn coolness of Maryland's boat-thick Chesapeake Bay? Manatees don't survive in water temperatures below 63 degrees.

A special Marine Animal Rescue Program boat and crew found the manatee, threw a net, and hoisted him out of the water. He moved into an isolation tank at the waterfront National Aquarium in Baltimore. There he munched fifty pounds of food a day, on the low end of normal for a manatee. Then on October 5, 1994, Chessie was taken from the National Aquarium and placed in a special ambulance to head to the airport. As the ambulance pulled away, police motorcycle escorts accompanied the manatee with lights flashing and sirens blaring! The team said it was worth the effort.

"There's so few of these animals left," said a spokeswoman for the National Aquarium, Vicki Aversa. "It's really important to get this one back to Florida." Manatees are not just curious critters to look at, they are also a species listed by the federal government as endangered, which is under review although advocates believe that is unwise.

At the airport Chessie's odd experience with humans wasn't over. He was wrapped into the flight deck of a U.S.

Coast Guard C-130 transport airplane. He flew to Orlando and was driven to SeaWorld, which also has a marine mammal rescue hospital and rehabilitation program. He received a medical checkup that showed him to be 10 feet long and 1,250 pounds. Despite his hours out of water, Chessie arrived safely home in Florida to swim again.

The total cost for the trip is hard to calculate, but an important private, nonprofit support group for manatees based in Florida, Save the Manatee Club, paid at least $7,000 of the expense. So with many people's help, Chessie became the first Florida manatee airlifted home and the first manatee to have a motorcycle police escort. And at that point, his swim to Maryland was also the farthest anyone knew a manatee would skedaddle.

By that next summer, 1995, when Chessie swam past Chesapeake Bay and all the way to Point Judith in Rhode Island, people knew they were dealing with an unusual critter. By now Chessie wore a special belt scientists had placed gently around his paddle-shaped tail. The belt was fitted with a floating tube tracking device, called a tag. It beamed radio signals with Chessie's location and even the nearby water temperature to polar orbiting satellites, which sent the information back to Earth. Chessie was one of about twenty manatees tracked this way, to learn more about their life in the wild.

As he swam through Connecticut waters that summer of 1995, Chessie lost the tracking device. The devices have a weak link that breaks loose if the tag gets tangled in something, such as the underwater part of a dock. Chessie's tag transmitter was found afloat near New Haven, Connecticut.

Sightings of Chessie by people along the Eastern Seaboard would now be the only way to pinpoint his location, said Diana Weaver as she asked the public to help that summer of 1995. She was a spokeswoman for the U.S. Fish and Wildlife Service, one of several agencies that is charged with protecting manatees.

# Scar Files

About 2,000 of the estimated 3,000 to 3,500 West Indian manatees in the wild in Florida, including Chessie, have snapshots on file of their distinctive scars for identification.

Manatees don't fight with each other, with humans, or with other animals. Scars result from wounds inflicted by impacts from water traffic. These collisions can kill manatees when they die immediately from the big smack of a high-speed boat hull or keel, or by a raking from large propellers. Or they can die later, from persistent deep-wound complications, such as infections and illness. The wounds can lower a manatee's resistance, allowing them to suffer lung ailments, such as pneumonia.

And that's exactly how people helped along the coast. At beaches and in boats, on fishing piers and from shore restaurants, reports of Chessie filtered in. People looked for a gray face sticking up out of the bay, a river, or inshore ocean water, a face with bristly whiskers and two round eyes, two round nose holes, and no visible ears. And if the manatee was close, they looked for a long scar down his back. They also resisted the urge to approach Chessie, which could interfere with his plant grazing and journey home.

Chessie's travel prompted questions. Why did he swim off to feed in distant, cooler waters? Some biologists thought he might have learned at least part of the route as a calf, alongside a well-traveled Florida mama.

And bay researcher Kent Mountford reminded the Alliance for Chesapeake Bay that in August 1980 a manatee was sighted near the Georgetown Canoe Club in Washington, D.C. Then, sadly, its body was found two months later. Specialists said pneumonia and starvation were the cause of death.

Other pre-Chessie manatee sightings had been rare but recorded in the Chesapeake region's waters as far back as 1676. Some of the sightings were the origins of beloved Chesapeake Bay "sea monster" stories.

Others said Chessie might like a particular food he found in northern grass beds, where the delicacies included pondweed, wild celery, widgeon grass, and eel grass, according to bay naturalist Kay Reshetiloff. Still others said Chessie was just a curious creature.

In Florida manatees group together during winter at warm-water sources. At any time of year they touch faces to each other and talk in squeaks underwater. But they also act quite independently, like Chessie.

Taking the slow way home in 1995 rather than the motorcycle escort/Coast Guard airplane route of 1994, reports of Chessie on a southward route were collected from fishermen, boaters, and a startled surfer. He showed up safely in Florida in November, after his historic 3,000-mile round trip.

The next year, 1996, Chessie left Florida waters for the north on June 12, according to the satellite tracking data collected by researchers such as Bob Bonde, with the Sirenia Project of the U.S.. Geological Survey in Gainesville, Florida. (Sirenia, the order in which manatees are classified, comes from the ancient word for "siren," a term for mytho-logical sea creatures that made sailors wreck.) In July 1996 Chessie fed in North Carolina. Then his tube transmitter was found July 17 near Beaufort, North Carolina. This was actually the third transmitter breakaway for Chessie. Biologist Jim Reid of the Sirenia Project said then, "We expect that Chessie is fine and continuing his travels north. He is probably continuing his ten- to twenty-mile-per-day travel rate as he works his way into Chesapeake Bay."

On September 23, 1996, Chessie was seen further north, in Virginia waters. And then to the delight of manatee trackers, he was back swimming in Florida near the Jacksonville Electric Authority's warm-water discharge on

November 16, 1996. He also surfaced in Florida waters on February 20, 1997.

Following the most publicity ever focused on a single manatee—the 1994 airlift, motorcycle escort, press conferences, e-mailed reports, and years of coastal lookouts—Chessie performed a disappearing act.

Season after season Chessie wasn't found, although there were unverified manatee sightings. Then in the summer of 2001 along Maryland's upper eastern shore of Chesapeake Bay, a pair of startled water-skiers said they saw a gray face in the water.

Again, the National Aquarium in Baltimore arrived on the scene. David Schofield, a marine mammal rescue coordinator with the aquarium, went to look. There, in Cornfield Creek, a tributary of the Sassafras River, Schofield confirmed a manatee sighting on August 23, 2001. But was it Chessie?

Then on August 30, 2001, engineers Rob Poyner and Joel Scussel were on duty at the Great Bridge Locks near Norfolk, Virginia, where thousands of boats gain access to the Chesapeake watershed. Boat locks are moveable gates separating water bodies, in this case a canal and a river tributary. Manatees must navigate through these big water gates that are in their migration path. Sometimes manatees are crushed in the locks. The two engineers looked down and saw a manatee waiting in the lock basin. They knew who to contact. Sue Barco, a marine mammal scientist at the Virginia Marine Science Museum, quickly brought over a research team. The manatee waited patiently, which told Barco this manatee had been through the lock process before. But was it Chessie? Careful photographs were taken. The lock gates opened and the mammal swam south.

In Gainesville, Florida, Cathy Beck, the photo chief for the Manatee Individual Photo-identification System, looked at the images and shared news. The manatee in the lock was Chessie. He had picked up more scars on his tail and back, she noted. But after five years, Beck said Chessie was back!

In huge part Chessie's story is so remarkable because he successfully maneuvered through areas of heavy traffic, including the waters of New Jersey and New York harbors. "I don't know how he traveled so far and got marked so little. He's a very wise animal," said Beck. Chessie is estimated to be thirty to fifty years old. Manatees can live to be fifty and even older.

## Adoption Option

The Save the Manatee Club, based in Florida, has information on how to "adopt" a manatee, plus cool manatee facts and information: www.savethemanatee.org.

# Mo the Manatee

Monica Ross, a scientist in Florida with Wildlife Trust and the Manatee Rehabilitation Partnership, which presents information at a Web site called Wildtracks.org knows Mo, a manatee orphan. Many students follow the scientist's engaging online diary about Mo's travels and victories.

Having become captive for his own safety in 1994 as an orphaned youth, without a real mom to show him the ropes of finding and eating his veggies, Mo understandably took awhile to learn how to live as a wild adult manatee. He has been cared for and learned skills at every manatee rehabilitation facility in the state.

His miscues have involved not eating enough, once almost to the point of emaciation, and swimming from a release area where researchers hoped to keep an eye on him, to miles from a shoreline in the Dry Tortugas. It took Mo three catches, retrainings, and releases before he got it right.

Although some students and families have helped researchers keep track of Mo, some members of the public have made mistakes with Mo, with no excuses. They've deliberately interfered with Mo's distinctive paddle-tail belt and tag that warns: manatee tag, do not touch. The tag transmits his location to Ross. In the winter of 2007, Ross saw five wildlife tour operators maneuver close to Mo so tourists could plop into the water and swim up to him. Ross asked the operators to keep customers away from Mo. Interference can prevent a manatee from getting enough underwater plant chow, among other harms.

"I'm proud of Mo," said Ross. His doctor, Tampa's Lowry Park Zoo vet David Murphy, and Ross cleared Mo to remain in the wild in the winter of 2007.

To learn more about Mo and the other manatees, Ross, and the Manatee Rehabilitation Partnership, visit www.wildlifetrust.org and www.wildtracks.org. To report manatee harassment or an injured manatee, see the "How to Assist Florida's Animals" section at the end of this book.

Since Chessie's trips more Florida manatees, a sub-species of the West Indian manatee, have been sighted in Northeastern states. Researchers theorize that such long trips may have been more common for manatees in previous centuries.

In 2002 a manatee with boat scars was seen in the Chesapeake area several times, but there was no reliable confirmation that it was Chessie. A manatee also was seen in Richmond, Virginia, waters the summer of 2002 by students of Virginia Commonwealth University professor Ralph Hambrick. He was taking them on a walking tour by the James River for his river policy course. It's not known if this was Chessie.

Other manatee sightings—at Sag Harbor in the Hamptons on the north shore of Long Island, at Virginia Beach and in Chesapeake Bay near the original capture sight of Chessie in 1994, and in the East River in New York City—tantalize researchers and the public.

"Unfortunately there's been no confirmed sighting" since the August 2001 news at the locks, said Cathy Beck. "I don't know where manatees go when they don't show up. Manatees have gone twelve years between confirmed sightings. We have no reason to think that Chessie is not out there, swimming."

For a list of Florida sites where you're likely to see manatees in the wild or in aquariums, see the "Snooty" chapter.

# SNOOTY: MANATEE MASCOT

t was sixty years ago and a beautiful time in Miami. Visitors and residents of the subtropics went about the job of exploring the sandy place. As they walked in neighborhoods past palm trees and orchid blooms, children heard the squawk of parrots on porches. They saw pelicans glide over the water. They watched a giant moon that seemed to rise right out of the Atlantic Ocean at Miami Beach. Curious families made their way to a small ship along Biscayne Bay, at a Fifth Street boat basin. They paid a fee and climbed aboard the ship.

The odd thing about this boat, the *Prins Valdemar,* was that it wasn't afloat in the bay. It was entirely propped up on land at this marina. Odder still, this ship was filled with fish—live fish.

The former schooner had been rearranged with concrete tanks in the staterooms to provide homes for seahorses, squid, and sea turtles. It was known as the Miami Aquarium.

According to the aquarium, one summer night in 1948, the old ship became an aquarium for the record books when the first manatee known to be born in captivity came into the world, inside the ship. It was recorded as July 21.

The wrinkled newborn tube of gray skin, fat, tissue, and a stubby, round face, with round eyes and nose holes like buttons, was called Baby Snoots by Miami's children. Later it was also called Little Snoots and Snooty.

Before his first birthday, Baby Snoots and thousands of marine animals that lived on board the ship faced eviction. A disagreement about the land and the condition of the ship meant that the shipboard aquarium would close. Zoos and other aquariums agreed to take some of the creatures.

Because Baby Snoots had been handled a lot by humans—probably bottle-fed and allowed to swim with children—it was decided to keep him captive when his mother, Lady, was returned to the wild.

At the time of the great animal adoption and release, Baby Snoots was across the state on the west coast. He was on display at a festival in Bradenton, south of Tampa. For 25 cents people peered into his tank. He had traveled across land from Miami to Bradenton "in the back of a pickup truck in a box of water," said his curator, Carol Audette. He survived the 220-mile trip on the Tamiami Trail through the Everglades and Big Cypress Swamp. That gave Baby Snoots the dubious distinction of being the first manatee to ride across the state like that.

People in Bradenton, which is in Manatee County,

thought they should adopt the young manatee because, after all, the mammal was their county's namesake.

So Baby Snoots, who needed a new home, became a mascot for Manatee County in 1949. He settled in, eventually living at Bradenton's South Florida Museum downtown near the Manatee River waterfront. Each time the museum grew and moved, the manatee from Miami did, too.

Snooty became a crowd-pleaser. It was one thing for children to know about sleek sharks they saw hanging up with the day's catch on fishing docks, or to be aware of dolphins, a mammal they saw splashing in the bay and Gulf waters. But few people had ever seen a manatee or had even known that these mammals still existed.

So Snooty served Florida as an early environmental educator. And he represented a history lesson, because manatees had been Florida natives for more than one million years.

In his early days in captivity Snooty munched on whatever greens were around. "They got scraps from stores. They knew it should be greens and not hot dogs or cold cuts," said Audette, a Rhode Island native who worked as Snooty's curator from 1984 to 2005. "But he did not grow. He grew slowly because of people not knowing the proper care. It's really kind of interesting that he has survived so long. I really think he is a strong animal with a strong will to live. He knows he has a job to do."

If you visited Snooty today you'd see that he did grow. He's about the length of a station wagon—9 feet, 4 inches long. But that isn't all there is to marvel about Snooty. He has his name registered as a trademark. He is thought to be the longest-living captive manatee in the world. His picture has appeared all over the world, at such places as the Learning Channel and the BBC television network. His visitors have included a vice president (Dan Quayle) and a children's television personality (Captain Kangaroo).

Like manatees in the wild, Snooty chows down. He eats eighty to ninety pounds of goodies a day. But his diet is different than the seabed grasses of wild manatees. The menu is apples, a Chinese lettuce called bok choy, sweet potatoes, cabbage, kale, carrots, romaine lettuce, collards, and store-bought vitamins.

Until the most recent years of his life, Snooty was a manatee without a social life. He knew only the human species. Because of his years of handling by people, "I think he probably would have picked humans first, over his own species," said Audette, who regularly greeted Snooty at about 3:00 a.m. to clean his pool and feed him.

*To report an injured or tagged manatee call (888) 404-3922.*

To interact with people, Snooty developed unusually strong muscles in his front flippers. He did this by repeatedly pushing up from his shallow, 4-foot pool bottom to perch partially out of the water, a characteristic Snooty pose.

But as awareness about the species and its needs increased, Snooty's handlers built him a deep, 60,000-gallon pool. Then he could receive manatee visitors—injured manatees that needed a safe place to recover from boat wounds or illness before returning to normal life.

What did Snooty think of the new pool pals? "At first he let them take away his food. Then he learned not to," Audette said. "He's learning to be more of a manatee."

Snooty sees a special vet, David Murphy, who visits poolside from the Lowry Park Zoo in Tampa, which works in

# You Can Go!

- Snooty's home is the Parker Manatee Aquarium at the South Florida Museum in Bradenton. Times of manatee education programs, which Snooty participates in, are listed on the Web site: www.southfloridamuseum.org.

- In winter months manatees seek warmer waters and often can been seen at:

**Blue Spring State Park:**
www.floridastateparks.org/bluespring

**Manatee Springs State Park:**
www.floridastateparks.org/manateesprings

**Merritt Island National Wildlife Refuge:**
www.fws.gov/merrittisland/

**Fort Pierce:** www.manateecenter.com

**Fort Myers:** www.leeparks.org

**Tampa:** www.tampaelectric.com/manatee

**Crystal River:** www.fws.gov/crystalriver/

**Homosassa Springs: ***
www.floridastateparks.org/homosassasprings

*\* Note: There is daily manatee-viewing because of the captive springs herd.*

Lucky canoeists can see manatees in warm-weather months in the Wakulla and St. Marks Rivers in North Florida near the St. Marks National Wildlife Refuge. The Humanatee Festival at St. Marks celebrates all the area's wildlife, especially the returning warm-weather manatees. Call (850) 925-6216 for information.

■ Several excellent sites specialize in caring for captive manatees, including those that are ill or injured and are expected to be released back to the wild:

**Lowry Park Zoo:** www.lowryparkzoo.com

**Mote Marine Laboratory and Aquarium:** www.mote.org

**SeaWorld:** www.seaworld.com

**Miami Seaquarium:** http://miamiseaquarium.com

**The Living Seas/Epcot:** www.wdwmagic.com/living.htm

**Parker Manatee Aquarium:** www.southfloridamuseum.org

■ These agencies also provide current manatee news:

**The Save the Manatee Club:** www.savethemanatee.org.

**The Florida Fish and Wildlife Conservation Commission:** www.myfwc.com/manatee/.

Read the amazing online diaries of several manatees released back into the wild, after treatment for illness or injuries: www.wildtracks.org.

more detail with captive manatees. Staff members hoist Snooty onto a sling scale for weigh-in. He tips the scales at 1,220 pounds. The doc takes blood and urine samples and tries to hear a heartbeat or pulse through the blubber. He checks for good breathing. Manatees can become sick with bronchitis, pneumonia, and other lung and respiratory problems. The only serious threat known through the years was a mechanical pencil he swallowed and it's still a mystery to this day where it came from. It gave Snooty a big bellyache in the 1970s and caused him to lose his appetite until Snooty passed it, in pieces, in his poop.

Snooty will celebrate his sixtieth birthday in 2008. The celebration will include "fruitcake" and lots of fun. Audette thinks Snooty is healthier today than when he was younger. "Over the years he's become more active. He does more swimming, more playing with other animals. His activity level is better. His prognosis is very good."

# JET: DOG NEAR THE RUNWAY

I't's a typical warm winter lunchtime in southwest Florida. Passengers in a jet are eager to land and drive over to lush Gulf of Mexico islands laced with sugar-sand beaches. The visitors disembark at the Southwest Florida International Airport. They pick up their luggage and head for their rental cars, unaware that a unique shaggy dog played a historic role in their safe landing.

Tucked away at the airport is a shaded memorial garden. It has a small bench and tranquil waterfall and a small marker for the grave of a dog named Jet.

This resort airport was the proving grounds in 1999 for an unusual experiment in aviation safety. It began here in February of that year with the arrival of a new employee who liked to play Frisbee during work and eat kibble afterward. But this airport employee really loved to chase after wild animals. His favorite thing to chase was birds.

His name was Jet.

Fortunately for Jet, this 450-acre airfield was home to a lot of birds—at least one hundred species. The airport was especially attractive to waterfowl such as ducks, as well as crows, blackbirds, and wading birds, including egrets and herons. They landed in flocks in the fields and at watery sites around the airport, and found these spots to be perfect feeding grounds. Once, tall sandhill cranes, an endangered species, had even walked out onto the runway. Some birds liked the airport so much they had even nested in the airfield.

To land and then take off, the airport flocks sometimes flew in the same airspace that jets and other aircraft did. The result of birds mingling with aircraft was unpleasant for the birds. Fortunately, a federal study reported that of sixteen confirmed bird strikes in 1998, none caused injury to humans. But the strikes were killing or at least hurting the birds, and causing aircraft damage and expense. Most important, every time a bird was struck it jeopardized human safety.

Airport senior operations manager Bobby Orick and planning and environmental compliance manager Jami McCormick wanted to reduce those bird strikes. The two staff members thought that by studying this bird problem they also could help birds in a region that was famed for its bird-watching, such as at the island's J. N. "Ding" Darling National Wildlife Refuge.

Jet's part of this story, as is often the case with amazing animals, begins with abandonment and a potential death sentence. An owner had left him at an animal shelter because he was considered too mean a canine to keep at home.

Grown-up dogs with rough reputations don't have much future once they are left at an animal shelter. But a dog trainer named Nicholas Carter actually was looking for border collies. An aggressive border collie was fine with him. He loved the breed and knew what they needed, to thrive and be happy.

The border collie isn't an animal to keep confined inside a house or an apartment. Border collies were bred in Scotland and England to herd sheep. They can easily run hundreds of miles a day. They love to herd almost anything. If they don't get the chance to run and herd, they become unhappy.

So Carter worked to rescue border collies from confinement in shelters, to train them for jobs doing what they loved to do. But sandy Florida isn't known for having many sheep to herd.

Jet was one of Carter's rescues. And by February 1999, after six to nine months of training near Gainesville, Jet was ready to work.

Trained border collies had already gone to work at golf courses to chase wild birds out of the way of golfers playing on fairways and at the putting holes. Jet was destined for something more.

As the airport completed its bird-strike study, manager Bobby Orick decided to hire Jet to chase birds. This made him the first dog in the United States to go to work in wildlife management at a commercial airport. His job would be to chase off the birds without harming them.

After watching him in practice, airport staff thought so highly of Jet's demonstrated skills, the airport paid $6,000 for him and the training. On February 11, 1999, Jet joined the airport's established security canines that already lived at the airport kennel as part of the official airport team. Several airport employees, called operations agents, met Jet, trained with him, and worked with him. But Jet picked out a special partner from all the others.

"I had seen pictures of him and thought he was just a big puppy dog," remembered operations agent Rebecca Stansifer-Haggie. "He came out of the kennel and acted like I was his long-lost buddy. He came over and put his feet up on me. He was licking my hands."

Over time Stansifer-Haggie became Jet's main partner. They made two trips a day in the airport's white Ford Explorer to restricted areas. Jet would ride out in his portable kennel, step out of it, and wait to be sent off on a voice or whistle command. He also chased the birds and returned from the chase on voice or whistle commands. He was trained to do this without a treat. To Jet it was treat enough to be alive and be *asked* to chase the birds.

A study after Jet had racked up months of work showed that bird strikes were significantly down. The flocks were fewer. They even began to fly off when they saw Jet's white Ford approach. The four-footed guy dressed in his shaggy black-and-white fur did the trick. In fact he was so good Jet began to get interested in herding alligators when the birds were gone. He went back to Border Collie Rescue for training so he would detour away from any alligator. The airport had experienced at least one alligator on the airport runway; a trapper took care of that wayward reptile.

When news got out about this unusual airport worker, Jet became a celebrity. Among his many honors, such as a nomination to an animal hall of fame and an award from the Cape Coral Chamber of Commerce, is a sheaf of mail from third-graders in Pennsylvania. They were so delighted by his shelter rescue and life story, they sent him a rawhide bone and hand-drawn pictures. Jet had his own business card, his own e-mail address, and a paw-print stamp for photos. His story appeared in magazines, on national news shows, and on Animal Planet's *K-9 to 5* and *Wild Rescues.*

Then Stansifer-Haggie started noticing her partner would become winded and tired out, when he hadn't before. An exam by his veterinarian, Sean Murphy, showed he had a heart defect; his heart valves were leaking blood. He was put on light duty in November 2000 and he met and helped teach his new friend and replacement border collie, Radar. Then in January 2001, two years after beginning work, Jet retired.

Fortunately for Jet, his favorite operations agent, Stansifer-Haggie, was a former vet assistant and zoo animal keeper. She owned a five-acre ranch occupied by dogs, a cat, and a horse. She offered him a home. Jet enjoyed an airport retirement press conference and heard many tributes before heading to retirement on her ranch.

# No dogs allowed?
## Dogs allowed!

More than ever before, dogs are allowed at work, because they work. An estimated 15,000 service dogs work in the United States, according to the thirty-year-old Delta Society, which advocates reliable training for pet-assisted therapy for humans.

Places where therapy dogs help people include: school classrooms, juvenile detention centers, mental health facilities, regular hospitals, hospice care centers, and nursing homes. In class the presence of a trained dog in her lap can help a reluctant student read "to the dog." Dogs encourage physical therapy patients to work harder. And they have lifted the spirits of depressed juvenile offenders and seriously injured Iraq war veterans.

Though many people know that dogs work on farms, in search and rescue missions, and for police agencies, dogs also just hang out when people work. Domino's Pizza headquarters is one large office among several that encourage workers to bring well-behaved pooches that know the "stay" command to doze by their humans' desks.

For more information on dogs and other pets at work, see www.deltasociety.org.

"We are all very sad to see one of the hardest-working—and most famous—airport employees leave," said Robert M. Ball, executive director of the airport authority.

Jet lived his last years in joy at the ranch. He even befriended a cat, Hitchhiker, that Stansifer-Haggie brought home from a vet's office where it had been dumped. The two critters eventually played cat chases dog and dog chases cat, in a friendly tumble on the ground.

To check his disease, Jet made visits to the experts at the University of Florida's College of Veterinary Medicine. But it was clear his heart condition, congestive heart failure, was worsening. He couldn't keep food in his stomach and his breathing was very difficult. He was euthanized, or put to sleep, in October 2003. He was eight years old—and amazing.

"He was a working partner," said a very sad but proud Stansifer-Haggie. "He could never be owned—just loved, respected, and cared for."

# ROSIE: BIG BEAUTY ON MIAMI BEACH

The elephant stood still. Four big, muscular legs supported this elephant's body. Its trunk moved slowly, like a boa. A boy stood transfixed, staring at the elephant on the Miami Beach polo-playing grounds this day in 1933. The boy was small, about 80 pounds. The elephant was built like an Army tank and weighed about 8,000 pounds.

So it was that the elephant named Rosie and the boy named Aristotle "Aris" Ares came together. No polo game was scheduled. But as was the case with Rosie, the resident elephant mascot of Miami Beach, people collected when she walked into view. Especially children.

Young Ares knew what would happen next. It was the habit of some beach boys to taunt other beach boys. "Everyone dares you to run under the elephant," he remembered of that day. He thinks he was about nine years old. "All the kids were pushing," he said. "You know how somebody pushes you toward an elephant?"

Actually, almost no one knows what it feels like to be pushed toward an elephant.

And to be taunted to do something crazy like run under the arch of its tall legs. (In Latin *elephant* means "huge arch.")

"Everyone dares you to run under the elephant," Ares, now a grown man, remembered. "So me—Joe Hero—that's what I do. I scrambled under Rosie to be the hero, never letting on my heart was beating a mile a minute. My heart jumped out of my mouth. I knew none of the children. My reward was the expression on their faces. I was a hero after that."

This Asian elephant, Rosie, didn't move. In fact she gave no sign that the boy dashing under her on a dare disturbed her. Rosie was famous for her sweetness. She was agreeable to having people hit golf balls off her back, and with people diving into pools from her back.

"She was gentle," remembered Robert Reilly, who, like Ares, enjoyed his childhood in Miami Beach in the late 1920s. Reilly celebrated his ninetieth birthday in 2006. And he still remembers that Rosie was sweet. "Anybody could walk up and pet her trunk and her legs. Every day Rosie was quite an attraction."

A developer of Miami Beach knew that if an elephant gave children birthday-party rides, pulled gondolas along the water, and planted coconut trees, those stunts would attract attention. And attention could increase sales of homes in the new city. That's how an elephant on the beach became a daily fact of life in south Florida.

No one bought a circus ticket to see Rosie. She was just there outside at the park, over at the polo-field grounds, along the waterfront—here, there, everywhere.

Rosie had an elephant pal, Carl II, also called Baby Carl and later renamed Nemo. The two elephants' days included whatever one of the area's big promoters and developers, Carl G. Fisher, wanted them to do. He owned the elephants. Their work included pulling gondolas, in a similar way that canal-boat mules and horses did in the northern United

States in such places as the Erie Canal. Fisher's elephants also pushed heavy concrete blocks, carried coconut trees to help plant them, and ripped out other trees (see Rosie's Lasting Legacy). They walked the golf course with clubs strapped to their sides, as "caddies."

# If You Go!

- To see Asian elephants, *Elephas maximus,* in Miami (and other fabulous animals of the world) visit the Miami Metro Zoo. Among its conservation projects, the zoo helps protect Asian elephants through anti-poaching patrols on the Indonesian island of Sumatra.

- You can visit the zoo's Asian elephant, Dahlip, and his companion, Nellie. For birthdays they enjoy giant Popsicles of apples and carrots. Dahlip has lived in Miami since 1967.

- All wild Asian elephants are endangered. They are smaller than African elephants and the males don't always have tusks.

- For more information see www.miamimetrozoo.com.

- Tampa's Busch Gardens features elephants, too. www.buschgardens.com

Fisher eventually sent Carl II/Nemo away, because this elephant showed a dislike for certain people, especially him. Once, wrote Fisher's wife, Jane, he knocked Carl Fisher down. And the famous developer foolishly grabbed Carl II's tail once, receiving a smack from Carl II's trunk.

Rosie apparently liked almost everybody, especially her gentle and skillful handler, Aaron Yarnell, whose previous expertise was with Georgia mules. A trainer brought over from Rosie's native India/Ceylon region was discharged mainly because Rosie refused to work with his techniques; she preferred gentle Yarnell. In a note to Fisher, Yarnell noted that some famous German circus owners had stopped by to admire Rosie. "Mr. Fisher, we have the greatest elephant in America," wrote her keeper.

"I don't know how her keeper got her to be so quiet, but she was regarded affectionately by the people on Miami Beach," said Reilly, thinking more than eighty years ago, when he was about seven years old and he often saw Rosie walking Miami Beach streets with her handler.

Rosie used her snaking trunk and big legs to help workers who made streets, and by lifting heavy blocks for buildings, into position. Once, standing patiently next to the open window of a local trolley car as Yarnell spoke with someone, Rosie poked her trunk in through the window. That woke up a sleeping passenger, who was so startled to find an elephant's trunk in his lap he broke his leg jumping out of the streetcar. He sued and was awarded $5,000 in damages from Fisher.

All other reports about Rosie's personal touch are glowing. She carried adults and children on her back. For publicity for a new golf course at Miami Beach, she let a man stand on her and hit a golf ball off her back and onto the golf green.

On another golfing occasion, after the country had elected Warren G. Harding to be the next U.S. president, he enjoyed a late-January vacation in Florida shortly before his inaugural ceremony in chilly Washington, D.C. While he was in Miami Beach, president-elect Harding played golf. Rosie worked as his caddy.

At other times for publicity Rosie walked to the edge of one of Fisher's pools and stood very still. Then swimmers would use Rosie's back as a diving board into the pool. Other times Rosie, who had been taught a tropical dance called the rhumba, would obligingly dance to music with Miami Beach visitors on the lawns of their hotels.

To bring more customers to a new bank, she walked right into the bank, stood before a teller's window, and handed the teller a bank deposit book with her trunk. Local legend has it that she also made her own "unplanned deposit" on Miami Beach First National Bank's marble floor. That brought a chuckle and even more attention.

As a child Reilly was so accustomed to seeing Rosie act friendly with so many people that when he went to a circus for the first time, he got in trouble because he walked right up to meet the big circus elephants without permission. He was just so familiar with Miami's elephant-about-town, Rosie.

Ares, the man who ran between Rosie's legs as a boy, has a second unusual connection to Rosie, because his father, Anatasios "Andy" Chakiris, worked for Fisher, the developer. One of his Chakiris's assignments was to hand concrete blocks and materials to Rosie, which she took where directed to help construct roads and buildings.

Although there are many photographs of Rosie helping people, it's hard to find images of people helping Rosie. For example, we aren't sure where she stayed in rough weather, such as hurricanes and bad storms, who her veterinarian was, or if she even had an animal doctor. Researcher Seth Bramson, a history teacher and author, thinks she may have stayed in a large dairy on Chase Street. Bramson said, "In a sense, Rosie *was* Miami Beach. She was photographed more than Carl Fisher was, and was known and loved by all of the children who came to the beach. She became a national icon and symbol of the beach."

Today, elders such as Reilly and Ares, and writers such as Bramson, know about Rosie. But there is little along Miami Beach streets to remind people that for a time the city's biggest resident, who was also a very gentle creature, walked and worked there. It appears there is no record that any street, building, or park was named for her, although she helped build many of them. Nor is there any sculpture dedicated to the big beauty.

What happened to Rosie in the next decades is an elephant-sized mystery. It's not likely that Rosie is still alive today. According to letters of Fisher, when his money situation turned out badly he decided he couldn't afford to keep her. A big responsibility of animal ownership is knowing in advance that you can find a safe new home when the animal can no longer be with you. When the animal is exotic and huge, the task is a big one. It's not known if anyone in

# Rosie's Lasting Legacy

In 2006 Rosie was in the news again after more than sixty years. Florida artist Xavier Cortada drew some of his inspiration for a community art project from a 1915 photograph of Rosie. The old image showed her with developer Carl Fisher, ripping out coastal forests of large mangrove trees. Mangroves and the life they support are a subject of Cortada's colorful large-scale paintings, including murals. Viewing the Rosie photo emphasized for him what Florida had lost, and it helped lead him to an idea.

Cortada decided to create a public art event, *The Reclamation Project,* to return some of the mangroves to the area. *The Reclamation Project* involved many people, including Key Biscayne Community School students, in tending for 2,500 live mangrove seedlings before their planting along the shore. An exhibit of the seedlings at Bass Museum and in many storefronts went up in 2006; the mangroves were planted in 2007.

In Rosie's day people thought mangrove forests were unhealthy. In our day it's proven that mangroves, which grow in tropical and subtropical parts of the world, actually filter pollution. Living right in the coastal water, these trees with exposed roots help keep the shores clean, provide living areas for fish, birds, and other animals, and they even build land.

Rosie could have planted a slender seedling herself. Elephant trunks are powerful but few people realize that a healthy elephant has so much control over her trunk's 40,000 muscles, she can pick up a feather or a mangrove seedling and deposit it uncrushed, wherever she wants. For what Rosie helped inspire, visit www .cortada.com.

Miami Beach wanted to take on the job of caring for Rosie. So how do you sell an elephant?

Rosie was offered to potential owners in several cities. In letters describing his elephant for sale, Fisher wrote that Rosie was "kind and gentle as a Newfoundland dog." He also said she would pull her own food in a cart and give herself a bath with a hose. "She has been photographed in possibly millions of films; rotogravure pictures by the thousands of feet have been run by all the newspapers in the country."

He also noted that for many weeks after a huge hurricane, she performed "Herculian labor that was equal to an experienced bunch of fifteen" human workers in straightening up trees and removing debris. He said she was thirteen years old, was nine feet high at her shoulders, and weighed four tons. He was asking $5,000 but he said he would drop the price to $2,500.

Jane Fisher wrote in her book that Rosie went to Atlanta. In 2000 a history of Zoo Atlanta said that a private Atlanta zoo helping stock the public zoo in 1935 sold an elephant named Rosie to a traveling circus show. Was this Rosie the same as Miami's Rosie? It's very likely. But there the elephant tale turns cold, until more research can pinpoint the story of that traveling circus show.

We do know that the famous Rosie left Miami Beach, where she made so many children happy. It's hard to hide an elephant, especially one as sweet and desirable as Rosie, so perhaps some day we'll know the rest of the story of Rosie, a big, sweet beauty on Miami Beach.

# BiG GUY: PANTHER PATiENT

I n 1981 Florida children voted that the Florida panther, a hunter of deer and wild hog that few people see in the wild, should be declared the official state animal.

At the time of the vote there were only about thirty left pawing through palmettos and wet prairie. They once had padded as far west as Mississippi and up into Tennessee. Now they hid out in extreme south Florida and were close to extinction.

"Every single panther was considered to be precious, important, and unique," *www.myfwc.com/panther* remembered Melody Roelke, a wild-animal veterinarian who specializes in the world's big cats.

The children's decision became law in 1982, and two years later a rare wild panther was slammed in traffic on a wetlands highway in a remote part of the state near the Everglades.

As it lay bleeding by the side of the road, traffic sped on through that night in November 1984, until truck driver Ronald Townsend saw the injured creature. Townsend interrupted his drive and tried to get the panther urgent help in the middle of the night.

Wildlife rescuers from many groups eventually arrived at the accident site along the two-lane road from Tampa to Miami, the Tamiami Trail. The hurt panther summoned strength. It crawled into a roadside canal to flee the people who brought help. Later the rescuers would understand what the panther's effort to crawl had involved; the animal had two broken hind legs, with bone showing through skin on one leg, a broken foot, and a split tongue.

The panther was darted with tranquilizer for safe handling as it clung to the highway canal bank, head above water. Strong rescuers in a boat held a net beneath the mammal so it wouldn't drown.

The costly battle to save this wild creature captured wide attention. For decades in Florida, ranchers and hunters had received government money, called a bounty, for every dead panther or its pelt they brought to town. Panthers were legally hunted in Florida until 1958, just twenty-six years before this highway collision. Illegal hunting of the panther continued even after the ban.

This panther for-the-record books was nicknamed Big Guy.

His first of many "firsts" was to travel by helicopter,

*Learn about an unusual world-class private animal preserve, White Oak Conservation Center, not open to the public. It's a haven for wild creatures, where Big Guy went to live. See www .giconline.org.*

head cradled in a veterinarian's lap, for emergency care at the nearest town, Naples. Then the injured panther traveled by small airplane about 400 miles north to

Gainesville and to the University of Florida's Veterinary Medical Teaching Hospital.

College animal surgeons familiar with farm animals and house pets operated on the wild feline to help his most-damaged leg and a foot.

"There was concern that he might not make it," remembered Jamie Bellah, one of the animal surgeons who helped. The panther survived. More operations over several days included screwing six steel plates into his legs to hold bone fractures together as they healed.

The team, including Bellah and Gail Donner, their colleague Mark Bloomberg, who has since passed away, medical manager George Kollias, and Melody Roelke, the wild feline expert, faced more challenges.

"You could not go in and examine and touch the incision, pick a leg up and move his joints, or do any kind of physical therapy," Bellah said. "One event I will never forget with Big Guy was the morning after the first surgery. . . . By the following morning, he had bent a plate about forty-five degrees by jumping on the one repaired leg, trying to get

## For Old Photographs and Anecdotes:

Caras, Roger. *Panther!* Boston: Little Brown & Co., 1969.

Tinsley, Jim Bob. *The Florida Panther*. St. Petersburg, Florida: Great Outdoors Publishing Co., 1970.

out of the pen he was confined to."

It was a shock and a dis-
appointment to all. "We had
never had a wild panther in
the vet school there," said
Roelke. "Nobody could appreciate the power and the
strength of this animal
despite what it had been
through."

*See the Florida Fish and Wildlife Con-
servation Commission's information on
panthers and read about the information
from transmission collars. Learn about
differences between the Florida panther
and the Florida bobcat, which people
understandably can mistake for the panther. Listen to Florida balladeer Dale
Crider sing about Big Guy through the
panther/handbook/natural life pages at
www.myfwc.com/panther.*

The panther was darted with medicine to make him
sleepy so he could be injected with a needle containing
anesthesia for more surgery. The rear leg that had been
repaired before was re-explored. The steel plate came out.
A new one, the size helpful to a horse, was inserted. Big
Guy also had his other rear leg repaired and he endured
more foot work. "This was pretty much an all-day affair and
despite this, his recovery was good," Bellah said.

When he was operated on the second time, wildlife
workers lowered the roof of his pen so he could no longer
do something cats do—jump.

But now Big Guy presented another surprise for his cap-
tors. He bit into the metal bars—repeatedly. "His canine
tooth just shattered. It split right off. He ended up fracturing
three or four canine teeth," Roelke remembered.

Fortunately, the year before, Roelke had moved twelve hundred miles from her zoo work in the Pacific Northwest to

# Panthers on the Prowl

- *Felis concolor coryi* is a distinct Florida panther subspecies of the mountain lion, known by about forty names, including cougar and puma in Western states and "painter" in Eastern states.

- The Florida panther is tan, never black.

- Parts of Florida were settled long after other U.S. regions. This, combined with the inhospitable climate (previously, no air conditioning, mosquito control, or hurricane forecasting) of South Florida, allowed panthers to keep retreating farther into a dense habitat as they were hunted. Today their last efforts to hide may not succeed, as people decide to live in panther territory.

- One male Florida panther needs a wild territory of about 250 square miles. Female panthers can make do with less.

Florida, just to study the Florida panther species. With her big-cat experience, she tried techniques on Big Guy that she had created working with cheetahs at Wildlife Safari in Oregon.

Big Guy ignored his food, hunks of deer meat. Roelke and the team helping Big Guy were worried. "He had lost a lot of blood. He was not eating," she said.

How to get an anemic, injured wild panther who had never before been in close proximity to humans to eat? Roelke held the meat on a hooked pole that she poked into his cage. "Then I would have to challenge him to hiss at me. If he would kind of hiss, I could poke the little chunk of meat into his mouth and he would eat it." Big Guy didn't know it, but his medicine was in the meat. Daily, repeatedly, this is how she tricked him into eating. He was released from the hospital to continue healing at a Florida Fish and Wildlife Commission animal enclosure in Gainesville. Roelke continued to work Big Guy back into semi-independence. She offered him small live animals, such as rabbit, for him to catch and eat.

Also, she tried a new tactic. First in the hospital and later at this enclosure, Roelke "spoke," or vocalized sounds in her throat that she had heard mother cheetahs make to their young in the Oregon zoo. To everyone's surprise, Big Guy answered Roelke regularly, becoming the first wild Florida panther documented to communicate repeatedly at length with a human this way. This incredible response-answer feat became part of a documentary video, *Edge of Extinction,* narrated by actress Loretta Swit.

Although Big Guy's injured teeth by now had been fixed with metal caps, it was doubtful that he could thrive when released back into the wild. In his grassy enclosure he had trouble killing a panther's common meal, a hog. And what would happen to him if his teeth caps popped out in the wild?

When Big Guy healed as much as possible, the private White Oak Conservation Center in North Florida offered him shelter in a new conservation program of world-class natural animal habitats. "He spent his last years there becoming as wild as possible again. The more space they gave him, the more wild he became," said Roelke, who visited him at White Oak.

Sadly, like many Florida panthers, Big Guy developed a brain disease that interfered with his walking and other important functions. He had to be euthanized, or put to sleep forever, on June 3, 1994, about ten years after his accident. Those involved with his story agree he never would have survived after that accident if the truck driver hadn't decided to help.

Big Guy had been about three, the age of a young adult male, when the accident forever altered his life. Panthers can live to age fourteen to sixteen in the wild, but more and more, extreme ages are less likely. Big Guy died at about age thirteen.

"He taught us a lot about how to rehabilitate these cats," Roelke said about her most famous animal patient. "Many cats hit after fared much better because of what we learned from him."

Big Guy's fame helped people realize that Florida's panthers soon will become extinct without drastic help.

His highway collision helped focus attention on innovative ways to help the cats breed and hunt in peace across

# You Can Go!

Each March Florida Panther Week educational events designed especially for children energize the mammal's youngest supporters. See www.panthersociety.org and www.napleszoo.com for details.

Florida zoos known for student education about Florida panthers include:

- Jacksonville Zoo Visit the Florida Wild Habitat and receive updates about the rare twin panther cubs rescued in 2005 and nursed to health at the zoo's hospital http://www.jaxzoo.org.

- Tallahassee Museum of History and Natural Science is celebrated for an unusual captive breeding pair, which live at the edge of a cypress swamp: www.tallahasseemuseum.org.

- The Lowry Park Zoo in Tampa wins national honors for being family friendly. It offers a highly regarded native Florida section, including a setting for Florida panthers: www.lowryparkzoo.com.

- The Naples Zoo celebrates Panther Week each March with special events. The zoo is a lush site that encompasses the historic Caribbean Gardens, with plantings dating to 1919 and history connected to Teddy Roosevelt, Thomas Edison, and others: www.napleszoo.com.

- Silver Springs, a longtime family attraction in central Florida at a famous clear-water spring, is home to a panter exhibit. www.silversprings.com.

native lands that are ribboned by speeding traffic and new homes. Today highway overpasses at likely animal crossings allow panthers and other wild creatures to avoid crossing deadly highways. They walk in tunnels directly underneath traffic. This helps reduce traffic accidents, which helps animals and humans.

They are Florida's most endangered animal. The estimated panther population in Florida is between eighty and one hundred panthers trying to hunt, with perhaps only fourteen to seventeen of those females that can raise young. It is thought a population of two hundred and forty is needed for survival. They fight with rattlesnakes, alligators, and other panthers over increasingly scarcer territory. They are killed on highways every year, and lose territory to new home and business construction in their territories. Many people worry about their extinction.

Children help by collecting Pennies for Panthers. The pennies add up to help provide hidden cameras for recording more information on the animals. This allows a panther walking by a camera site, such as in an animal-path underpass, to trip the video and record its own image, such as a cute panther cub following behind a mama panther at night. All this, because of the airlift, operations, recovery, and retirement at White Oak for Big Guy, an amazing panther patient.

# Where Can I See a Wild Panther?

The Florida Panther National Wildlife Refuge is near Naples, but panthers there aren't ever exhibited. It's also unlikely you'll see these creatures in the wild. The Duncan Memorial Trail invites limited dawn-to-dusk refuge access on a boardwalk. Otherwise, except for a day in October to celebrate the national refuge system, the refuge is closed so the rare panthers have some chance of surviving extinction. The refuge explains its unusual mission at www.fws.gov/floridapanther.

The very active Friends of the Florida Panther Refuge invite membership, schedule education events, raise money to help monitor the panthers, and operate an informative site: www.florida panther.org.

For information on how to get help for any injured wild animal, see "How to Assist Florida's Animals" at the back of the book.

# Panther Posse

Students can set up an original Florida Panther Posse. Each class posse monitors radio-collared panthers and raises money for their assistance, including monitoring by panther-tripped video cameras.

Accurate panther news—births, panther fight fatalities, highway accidents—is delivered to posse schools from Wings of Hope, an award-winning program at Florida Gulf Coast University. The program receives information from the Florida Fish and Wildlife Conservation Commission and the Florida Panther National Wildlife Refuge, and shares it with children. For information visit www .floridapanther.org at the Panther Tales pages.

# APPENDIX A:
# MORE OF FLORIDA'S
# FAMOUS ANIMALS

Florida is a menagerie of even more animals. Step this way to see a few:

**Alligator:** (Wakulla Springs) Old Joe's dead, on view, with the murder never solved. Edward Ball Wakulla Springs State Park, www.floridastateparks.org/wakullasprings. Spend the night on the Big Cypress Reservation with the Seminole Tribe of Florida and see an alligator show: www.semtribe .com/safari/activities.

**Cats:** Ragamuffin and Pablo Picasso are among the 60 or so house cats lazing about at The Hemingway Home in the Keys. Known for their extra toes. www.hemingwayhome.com

**Buffaloes:** (Gainesville) Yes, they were here first. And once locally extinct, they are here again. Paynes Prairie State Preserve, www.floridastateparks.org/paynesprairie.

**Chickens:** (Cross Creek) Scratching in the yard, like when Pulitzer Prize–winning author Marjorie Kinnan Rawlings of *The Yearling* lived here. Rawlings House/Farm Yard National Historic Site: www.floridastateparks.org/marjoriekinnanrawlings.

**Dog:** (Tallahassee) Lichgate House, built in the style of a Hansel & Gretel cottage, is a National Register of Historic Places park site, with a matching dog house that once indulged Kip, a bulldog owned by the late classics professor Laura Jepsen: (859) 386-6556. www.lichgate.com.

**Flamingoes:** (Sarasota, Tampa) Sarasota Jungle Gardens features a stroll with flamingoes, and Busch Gardens/Tampa Bay hosts a signature flock. www.sarasotajunglegardens.com and www.buschgardens.com/BGT.

**Horses:** (Archer) Some beauties gave birth to well-known racers and were destined for slaughter. Others were left to starve in the Everglades. All are loved at Mill Creek Retirement Farm: www.millcreekfarm.org. Europe's famed Lipizzan horses with World War II heritage are based east of Sarasota: www.hlipizzans.com.

**Key Deer:** (Big Pine Key) Slow down in the Keys for these little Bambis. Key Deer National Wildlife Refuge: www.fws.gov/nationalkeydeer; visit injured cuties that can't return to the wild: Homosassa Springs Wildlife State Park: www.floridastateparks.org/homosassasprings.

**Mammoth/mastodons:** (Tallahassee, Gainesville) Henry strikes a toothy pose at the Museum of Florida History, reminding us of Florida's saber-tooth cat and tusker days. His bony cousins from the Aucilla River Prehistory Project tower at the Florida Museum of Natural History: www.flheritage .com/museum and www.flmnh.fl.edu.

**Monkeys:** (Silver River) Don't feed these river-roamers! Visit www.silversprings.com.

**Orangutans:** (Wauchula) Cute as baby actors, unwanted as big adults, loved here. Members can visit. Center for Great Apes: www.prime-apes.org.

**Red wolves:** (Tallahassee/Franklin County) Uncommon breeding program for this rare canine. Tallahassee Museum of History and Natural Science and at St. Vincent National Wildlife Refuge: www.tallahasseemuseum.org and www.fws .gov/saintvincent.

**Sharks:** (Sarasota) Noted for the study of sharks when no one would touch the topic, the Mote Marine Laboratory and Aquarium presents the best shark education program around: www.mote.org. For a dive on the wild side, swim with the sharks (restrictions apply) in Tampa at The Florida Aquarium: www.flaquarium.org.

**Space chimpanzees:** (Fort Pierce) Closed to the public but read the Web pages, especially the history on Enos, Ham, and colleagues. Center for Captive Chimpanzee Care: www.savethechimps.org.

**White squirrels:** (Sopchoppy/Tallahassee) Don't tell your parents and they'll do a double-take if they see these free-roaming cuties. Ochlockonee River State Park and the Tallahassee Museum of History and Natural Science: www .floridastateparks.org/ochlockoneeriver, www.tallahassee museum.org, and www.whitesquirrelinstitute.com.

**Whooping cranes:** (Central Florida) World-famous flock, of ultralight-aircraft video fame and 2007 tornado tragedy, attempting a comeback: www.operationmigration.org.

# APPENDIX B: HOW TO ASSIST FLORIDA'S ANIMALS

Animals deserve protection. Neglect, abuse, illegal fishing and hunting, harassment, or other violations, such as attempted capture of wild and protected species, should be reported. Most birds also are protected by state and federal laws, and hunters must have current licenses. There is never a valid reason for the harm of any animal, even a common species.

Reduce animal entanglement in trash by picking up land and shore litter. Never throw out fishing line, six-pack drink holders, or plastic bags. Groups involved in clean up of shore litter are Keep Florida Beautiful and The Ocean Conservancy.

**Domestic Pets, Farm Animals, or Captive Creatures, such as Circus Animals**

Details about animal mistreatment can be given to the police or sheriff's department (use the nonemergency telephone number, unless a severe violation is happening the moment you call), the public animal-control staff or shelter, or private nonprofit shelters such as the area's humane society. See lists of Florida humane societies and Florida County animal shelters at http://flarescue.tripod.com/humane.html.

Updates on selected Florida animal situations are at News for Florida Animal Advocates, www.blog.animalrights florida.org/.

## Wild Critters

Some wild species in Florida are covered by specific protections. For example, marine mammals such as dolphins, manatees, and whales are covered by the U.S. Marine Mammal Protection Act, and migratory birds, from small songbirds to large cranes, the wood stork, and eagles, are covered by the Migratory Bird Act.

The U.S. Fish and Wildlife Service receives reports of federal wildlife violations by region, via e-mail. Listings are at www.fws.gov/southeast/law/reportviolation.htm.

You also can telephone your regional U.S. Fish and Wildlife Service office, found in the U.S. Government listings in the phone book. Violations within a national refuge can be reported to the refuge staff and likewise at national parks.

## Alligators

It is always illegal to feed wild alligators, whether on private property, at a town park, or in wilderness. Always report people who feed wild alligators; this could save a child's life or that of a beloved pet. It can also help an alligator stay wild.

Nuisance Alligator Reports: (866) 392-4285 (866-FWC-GATOR)

Don't swim with alligators. Most Florida lakes, ponds, canals, and rivers are likely habitats for alligators. Beware if you are in an area without a lifeguard, and beware even if a lifeguard is present.

**Dolphins, Manatees, Sea Turtles, and Whales**

Don't swim with wild dolphins, manatees, sea turtles, or whales; it's harassment.

Call the Manatee Hotline, (888) 404-3922, to report entanglement, harassment, or tagged manatee locations.

To report entangled right whales or other seasonal (winter) right whale sightings from Brevard County northward, on Florida's east coast, call the Endangered Right Whale Hotline, (888) 979-4253.

**Report Other Animal Problems on Public Lands**

At a Florida state park or greenway, contact park staff and the Park Watch Program, (866) PARK-COP.

The Florida Fish and Wildlife Conservation Commission, which oversees Park Watch, also operates Wildlife Alert. To report wildlife violations at any Florida location, call (888) 404-3922 (this is also the Manatee Hotline).

**Sick, Injured, or Orphaned Wildlife?**

One respected Florida wildlife group that posts detailed tips on dealing with wildlife in trouble is the Humane Association of Wildlife Kare and Education (HAWKE), www.hawkewildlife

.org. Otters are among the group's specialties.

Another well-known responder is the St. Francis Wildlife Association, which provides rescue tips on its Web site, www.stfranciswildlife.org.

Keeping wild birds or mammals as pets is illegal without a federal license.

*Never touch* a wild species that can carry rabies, even the babies. This includes: foxes, raccoons, and bats.

Area wildlife rescue societies take in injured creatures in hopes of returning them to the wild after they heal. Local animal shelters usually have the names of wildlife rescuers in the area to call about an injured creature.

Rescue group contacts are also at the Wildlife Rehabilitation Information Directory, www.tc.umn.edu/~devo 0028/ and also www.southeasternoutdoors.com/wildlife/ rehabilitators/index-rehabilitators.html

**Exotics**

Exotic pets can lead to exotic problems. Animals living here that aren't native to Florida include Burmese pythons illegally let loose. They famously tangled with alligators in the Everglades in 2006.

It is never legal to release exotic creatures, which some people think make great pets until they find they can't handle them as they grow.

Details about release of exotic animals should be reported to federal Fish and Wildlife Service and Florida Fish and Wildlife Conservation Commission officers.

Exotic animals require a specialized diet, care, and time for proper health—a huge expense.

Nonnative Pet Amnesty Day in Clearwater, Florida, took place in March 2007 to provide a humane way to place unwanted nonnative pets up for adoption, with no questions asked. For information visit myfwc.com/nonnatives/AmnestyDay.html.

For information on problems with exotic big cats kept as pets in Florida, see http://bigcatrescue.org.

*Note:* Animal rescue organization Web sites may contain pages with images of animal injuries from rescue or in recovery; adults may want to preview before students research these sites.

# APPENDIX C: SOURCES

**Maya: Mystery Owl**

Beck, Sandy. Interviews with author, March 10 and May 1, 2006.

———. "Mystery Bird Lands in Tallahassee." *Wildlife Matters* 4, no. 1, winter 2006. Quarterly newsletter of the St. Francis Wildlife Association, P.O. Box 38160, Tallahassee, FL 32315; www.stfranciswildlife.org.

Jue, Dean. E-mail with author, May 22, 2006.

Pranty, Bill. "Eastern Screech Owl," *Florida's Breeding Bird Atlas* site, http://myfwc.com/bba/EASO.htm.

Sullivan, Barbara. Conversations with author, March 10 and May 1, 2006.

Wild Classroom Web site, www.thewildclassroom.com.

**Dave: Parade Cat**

Alexander, Mike. "Mime Troupe Was Unique." *Tallahassee Democrat,* April 1989.

Anderson, Nancy. "The Catman Has Enjoyed Parading in the Big Bend." "Ask Nancy" pet column, *Tallahassee Democrat,* 1999.

Jason, Lauren. "Parade Provided Tribute to Past." *Tallahassee Democrat,* November 1988.

Gans, Mitch. Interview with author, Tallahassee, Florida, January 2, 2006.

Ruth, Paul. "A Fun-filled day." *Tallahassee Democrat,* August 3, 1988.

**Boo Boo: Capital Bear**

Breault, Tim. Interview with author, Tallahassee, Florida, September 9, 2005.

Brewer, Bruce. "The Fall of the Wild: Boo Boo's Big Adventure." *Tallahassee Democrat,* August 2, 1996.

——. "Cub Can't Bear It: Bye-Bye Boo Boo." *Tallahassee Democrat,* August 1, 1996.

Cabbage, Henry. Interview with author, Tallahassee, Florida, September 9, 2005.

Florida Fish and Wildlife Conservation Commission. Black Bear and Education pages at http://myfwc.com.

Greene, Juanita. "Florida's Battered Bruins." *Defenders,* spring 1993.

Johnson, David. Interview with author, Tallahassee, Florida, September 13, 2005.

Siebert, Steve. "The Apalachicola Black Bear." *Florida Wildlife* 51, no. 4; 16–17.

Weaver, Dennis. www.dennisweaver.com.

## Electra: Manatee Aided by Manatees

Dietz, Tim. *The Call of the Siren.* Golden, Colo.: Fulcrum Publishing, 1992.

Endangered Species Program. United States Fish & Wildlife Service. www.fws.gov/endangered.

Hughes, Marianne and Neil. Interview with author, May 13, 2006.

Homosassa Springs Wildlife State Park. http://florida stateparks/homosassasprings.

Horikoshi, Chifuyu. E-mail and telephone conversation with author, April 13–15, 2006.

Jacobs, Francine. *Sam the Sea Cow.* New York: Walker & Co., 1991. (Originally published as *Sewer Sam, the Sea Cow,* 1979.)

Robinson, Matt. Manatee education presentation, interview with author, May 13, 2006.

Strawbridge, Susan. Telephone conversation with author, April 11, 2006.

St. Petersburg Times. "Refuge Greets Deer and Manatee." May 23, 2000.

Tallahassee Democrat. "The Real Florida: Homosassa Springs Park Draws Crowds." March 27, 2006.

**Lu: Town Hippo**

Clarke, Lynn. E-mail interviews with author, April 25, May 9, and May 17, 2006.

Strawbridge, Susan. Telephone interview with author, April 11, 2006, and e-mail message and attachments, April 20, 2006.

The Wildlife Connection 3, no. 11, Crystal River, Florida, February 2006.

Zoological Society of San Diego, public relations department spokesperson, e-mail to author about birth date of hippo born to Rube and Lotus, May 23–24, 2006.

**Sunset Sam: Dolphin Deeds**

Chiu, Faye. "Healing Partnerships." Animal Assisted Therapy page, Petfinder Library: www.petfinder.com.

Clearwater Marine Aquarium. www.cmaquarium.org.

Cyber Animal Art Show. www.gettheloop.com/artshow/
analysis.html.

Deggans, Eric. "Animal Love, Human Healing." *St. Petersburg
Times,* June 28, 1998.

Stone, Abigale. Telephone interview with author, June 6,
2006.

**Flipper**

Gray, William B. *Flipper the Star.* Miami: E. A. Seeman
Publishing, 1973.

Plummer, Joseph. "Heart Attack Kills Original Flipper." *St.
Petersburg Times,* July 15, 1971.

Santini's Porpoise Training School advertisement, author's
collection.

**Nellie**

First Coast News. www.firstcoastnews.com, March 1, 2007.

Marineland Dolphin Conservation Center. www.marineland
.net.

**Tamani: 205-Pound Newborn**

Eichler, Sarah. Telephone conversations with author, April 27
and May 7, 2006.

LeFave, Steve. Telephone interview with author, May 2006.

Lowry Park Zoo. Rachel F. Nelson, zoo spokeswoman. Telephone conversations and e-mail with author, May 2006.

Zayas, Alexandra. "Elephant Calf Christened at Lowry Park Zoo." *St. Petersburg Times,* December 22, 2005.

## Brownie: Dog for All of Daytona

Associated Press. "City Honors Deceased Town Dog." *Florida Times-Union,* Jacksonville, May 4, 1994.

*Daytona Beach News-Journal.* "Brownie Dies; He'll Be Buried in Park." November 1, 1954.

Ellis, Joan. "Daytona Then and Now," letter to the editor. *Daytona Beach News-Journal,* February 12, 1989.

Halifax Historical Society vertical files, Daytona Beach.

Hunter, Robert. "Two Dogs that Captured City's Heart." *Daytona Beach News-Journal,* July 5, 1992.

Langworthy, Fred. "Outdoors with Fred Langworthy." *Daytona Beach Sunday News-Journal,* November 7, 1954.

Sandler, Roberta. "A Dog's Home Is Many Hearths." *Our Best Friends: Wagging Tales to Warm the Heart,* ed. Michael Capuzzo. New York: Bantam, 1999.

Strickland, Martha Sue. "Dog Who Has Bank Account." *Atlanta Journal-Constitution,* June 1952.

Troy, Jack. "Friendly Dog Becomes City's Pet and Lives Like Royalty." *Jacksonville Times-Union,* February 6, 1949.

Vining, Keith. "Brownie Doesn't Live Here Anymore." Halifax Historical Society archives, undated, published magazine article.

## Chessie: Cold-water Visitor

Alliance for the Chesapeake Bay. *Bay Journal,* November 2001, September 1997, September 1996, July/August 1996, March 1996, September, 1995, July/August 1995. 6600 York Road, Suite 100, Baltimore, MD 21212. www .alliancechesbay.org.

Amato, Carol A., and David Wenzel. *Chessie, the Meandering Manatee.* Hauppauge, New York: Barron's Young Readers Series, 1996.

Beck, Cathy. Sirenia Project, Manatee Individual Photo-identification System, U.S. Geological Survey, Florida Integrated Science Center, Gainesville. E-mail with author, May 30, 2006, and conversation with author, May 25, 2006.

Bonde, Bob. "Helping Manatees Helps the Planet." *St. Petersburg Times,* January 2004.

Houk, Randy, and Paula Bartlett. *Chessie, the Travelin' Man.* Washington, D.C.: Humane Society of the United States Animal Tales Series, 1997. www.hsus.org.

Florida Fish and Wildlife Conservation Commission. Manatee pages and printable materials. www.myfwc.com/manatee.

Godown, Jan. "Propellers Still Threaten the Plant-munching Manatee." *Tallahassee Democrat,* October 20, 1985.

Hubbs-SeaWorld Research Institute. www.hswri.org.

National Aquarium in Baltimore. www.aqua.org.

Pittman, Craig. "Commission Looks at Manatee Protections." *St. Petersburg Times/Tallahassee Democrat,* May 31, 2006.

Reep, R. L., and R. K. Bonde. *The Florida Manatee: Biology and Conservation.* Gainesville: University Press of Florida, 2006.

**Snooty: Manatee Mascot**

Audette, Carol. Interview with author, October 24, 2005.

Luckhardt, Alice L. "*Prins Valdemar:* Glory to Tragedy." *Florida Monthly,* January 2005.

Save the Manatee Club. "Manatees: An Educator's Guide." Maitland, Fla.: U.S. Marine Mammal Commission.

"Snooty the Sea Cow Turns 51." *Bradenton Herald/Tallahassee Democrat,* August 2, 1999.

Stewart, Doug. "Making Sense of Manatees." *National Wildlife Magazine*, October/November 2005.

## Jet: Dog Near the Runway

Ryan, Laska. "Border Collie Helps Manage Wildlife at SWFIA." *Florida Flyer,* summer 2004.

Southwest Florida International Airport. www.flylcpa.com.

"Southwest Florida International Airport's Former Bird Dog Passes Away at Age 8." Press release, Southwest Florida International Airport, Fort Myers, October 8, 2003.

Stansifer-Haggie, Rebecca. Telephone interviews with author, December 22, 2005, and January 19 and 20, 2006.

"Wildlife Operations Agent Jet A. Dawg Retires from Southwest Florida International Airport." Press release, Southwest Florida International Airport, Fort Myers, January 11, 2001.

## Rosie: Big Beauty on Miami Beach

Ares, Aristotle. Telephone interview with author, April 14, 2006.

# Appendix C: Sources

*Atlanta History: A Journal of Georgia and the South* 43, no. 4, Zoo Atlanta Issue, winter 2000.

Bramson, Seth. E-mail interview with author, April 14, 2006.

Davis, Mark J. *Mr. Miami Beach: The Remarkable Story of Carl Fisher.* The American Experience, PBS Home Video, WGBH, Boston, 1998.

Fisher, Carl. Letters, telegrams 1921–1932, Carl Fisher document boxes, Research Center, Historical Association of Southwest Florida/Historical Museum of Southern Florida, Miami.

Fisher, Jane. *Fabulous Hoosier: A Story of American Achievement.* Chicago: Harry Coleman & Company, 1953.

Fisher, Jerry M. *The Pacesetter: The Untold Story of Carl G. Fisher.* Fort Bragg, California: Lost Coast Press, 1998.

Foster, Mark S. *Castles in the Sand: The Life and Times of Carl Graham Fisher.* Gainesville: University Press of Florida, 2000.

Hatfield, Liliam. Miami Beach City Clerk's Office. E-mail to author, April 13, 2006. www.miamibeachfl.gov.

Kleinberg, Howard. *Miami Beach: A History.* Miami: Centennial Press, 1994.

Laurel, Leff. "Early Promoters used beasts as well as beauties." *Miami Herald*, July 19, 1982.

Redford, Polly. *Billion-dollar Sandbar: A Biography of Miami Beach*. New York: E. P. Dutton, 1971.

Reilly, Robert. Telephone interview with author, April 12, 2006.

Zayas, Alexandra. "Biscayne Park History: Ahead of Its Time." Our National Parks journalism program feature-writing project, University of Miami School of Communication, May 6, 2004. http://com.miami.edu/parks/bishistory.htm.

**Big Guy: Panther Patient**

Alvarez, Ken. "Twilight of the Panther." Sarasota, Fla.: Myakka River Publishing, 1993.

Bellah, Dr. Jamie. E-mail correspondence with author, December 2005–February 2006.

Bransilver, Connie, and Larry Richardson, foreword by Jane Goodall. *Florida's Unsung Wilderness: The Swamps*. Englewood, Colo.: Westcliffe Publishers, 2000.

Fergus, Charles. "Swamp Screamer: At Large with the Florida Panther." New York: North Point Press/Farrar, Straus & Giroux, 1996.

*Gainesville Sun.* "Big Guy Well Enough for Outdoors." December 11, 1984.

Greene, Juanita. "Panthers at the Vanishing Point." *National Parks*, Washington, D.C., July/August 1985.

Maehr, David S. "The Florida Panther: Life and Death of a Vanishing Carnivore." Washington, D.C.: Island Press, 1997.

*On the Edge of Extinction: Panthers and Cheetahs.* Loretta Swit, narrator. Audubon Video, 1989.

Roelke, Dr. Melody. Telephone interview with author, February 9, 2006.

Rutan, Stephanie. E-mail correspondence with author, February 13 and 23, 2006.

"Saving the Last of a Vanishing Breed." University of Florida Health Science Center Annual Report, Gainesville, 1986.

*Wall Street Journal.* "Call of the Wild: Struggle to Save the Florida Panther." April 9, 1985.

# INDEX

# Index

# Index

# ABOUT THE AUTHOR

J G Annino is a spider wrangler who grows the mysterious hurricane lily in Leon County, Florida, where she lives with her family and with Ginger, the ladder-loving cat and Florida panther look-alike. JG has babysat a mynah bird, met a black bear on a trail, and photographed a pet Florida panther as it raced toward her.

Her favorite Florida animal species is the angel wing. Although not a cuddly critter, its skeleton is a joy to behold, if not taken live, but found naturally upon a beach. Her second favorite Florida animal is Henry, a North Florida unwooly mammoth she met in 1980 and visits several times a year.